CHRIS O'LEARY

PUBLIC SERVICE MOTIVATION?

Rethinking What Motivates Public Actors

POLICY PRESS SHORTS RESEARCH

First published in Great Britain in 2022 by

Policy Press, an imprint of
Bristol University Press
University of Bristol
1–9 Old Park Hill
Bristol
BS2 8BB
UK
t: +44 (0)117 374 6645
e: bup-info@bristol.ac.uk

Details of international sales and distribution partners are available at
policy.bristoluniversitypress.co.uk

British Library Cataloguing in Publication Data
A catalogue record for this book is available from the British Library

ISBN 978-1-4473-6079-7 hardcover
ISBN 978-1-4473-6080-3 ePub
ISBN 978-1-4473-6081-0 ePdf

Cover design: Bristol University Press
Front cover image: DESKCUBE / istock

Printed and bound by CPI Group (UK) Ltd, Croydon, CR0 4YY

This book is dedicated to my parents, whose support and encouragement has been constant and unconditional. A special thanks also goes to Hector and Hera, for making me laugh just when I need it.

Contents

List of figures and tables   vi

Preface   vii

one   Introduction   1

Part I   A critique of public service motivation theory

two   Conceptualising public service motivation   25

three   The public in public service motivation theory   51

four   Decision-making in public service motivation theory   73

five   Observing public service motivation   87

Part II   Expressively motivated public employees

six   Rationality, expressive interests and public service motivation   105

seven   Conclusion   137

Appendix   143

References   152

Index   171

List of figures and tables

Figures

5.1	Count of articles published by journal in 2020	90
5.2	Number of articles by region, and whether quantitative or qualitative in design	91

Tables

2.1	Attraction to public policy making and commitment to public interest	33
4.1	Comparison of bureau-shaping and public service motivation assumptions	81
6.1	The different rational motives of public employees	116
6.2	Expectations of expressively motivated public employees	132
Appendix	Articles published in 2020 containing 'public service motivation' in title	144

Preface

Before I entered academia, I was a civil servant in the UK. I spent five years as a policy director in an executive Non-Departmental Public Body that was responsible for regulating a healthcare profession. As I joined this agency, the UK government announced its abolition and transfer of its responsibilities to a successor body.

Rational choice theory predicts that, when faced with the threat of agency death, civil servants will seek to create coalitions with agency beneficiaries to prevent termination. Agency staff will seek to further their own interests – continued employment and pay – regardless of any public interest that might arise from the change. And yet, following some initial hesitation by the agency's board and significant opposition from professional bodies and service providers, the agency went on to become a keen advocate of, and played an instrumental role in, its own demise.

In public, the agency couched this in terms of the public benefit of improved public protection for patients, and reduced costs to the public purse. It also made clear that there were benefits to the regulated profession. Those opposed to the change also framed their arguments as being in the public interest. At one public meeting I attended to talk through the proposals, one member of the regulated profession commented that the agency was 'turkeys voting for Christmas' because of its advocacy of its own demise. But while the collective, public account of these changes were always advocated in the public interest, individual staff and board members also saw the benefits to them, individually. The challenges of proposing, managing and implementing policy change that involve closing down a public body, the potential career benefits, as well as what being involved would signal about their values, especially that they put the public interest of abolition ahead of the perceived self-interest of opposing abolition. Those who initially opposed the abolition also had self-interested reasons for doing so, not least because of the greater role that resulted for the professional bodies involved.

This mixture of self- and public interest motives, with individual and collective consequences, fascinated me. I went on to empirically examine the motivations of actors involved in policy change in my PhD thesis, and to also publish on agency termination.

It was through my PhD research that I first started to explore public service motivation theory (from here on in, abbreviated as PSMT). Unlike many of the theories in the social sciences I had previously studied, PSMT had a significant body of empirical evidence – and the type of empirical evidence I generally find convincing – to back it up. But the more I researched and the more I read, the greater the number of questions I had about the theory and its empirics. There were significant areas of disagreement within the field, areas which did not quite stack up, contradictory findings and a significant reliance on self-reported measures of both independent and dependent variables of interest. And, most significantly, there was little exploration of what is meant by the public interest, how civil servants might conceptualise and operationalise this, and how civil servants might deal with a clash between the interests of different publics. My empirical research – a survey of staff and students at my university, document analysis, budgetary analysis and interviews – found little evidence to support the theory, beyond the fact that, when asked, civil servants did indeed say they worked to further the public interest.

My academic work now involves policy analysis and policy evaluation. This is not directly about public service motivation, but inevitably, the motives of policy makers, service providers and others do come to the fore. And following the publication of my critique of PSMT in 2019 in *Public Personnel Management* journal, I wanted to further examine and critically evaluate PSMT.

The result is this book. Its aim is not to deny that public employees – like everyone else – have other regarding motives. But I do critique PSMT. I set out a number of issues with PSMT, including several areas where it offers little or no explanation. In doing so, I build on the (to date) limited criticisms in the literature. I also critically examine the empirical research on public service motivation, of which there is an impressive and ever-growing body of research.

The second and more substantive aim of this book is to provide an alternative explanation of what motivates public employees. This alternative theory is rooted in rational choice theory, proposing that expressive motivation explains the motives of those who work in the public sector.

Chris O'Leary

ONE

Introduction

The call of public service

That people are motivated to work for the public interest, for the good of others, for the betterment of society, is a long standing and appealing idea. It has been core to the writings of political philosophers in ancient Greece and Rome, in Medieval times and through to modern times (O'Toole, 2006) This simple proposition is repeated in works as diverse as Plato's *The Republic* (1987) and Woodrow Wilson's *The study of administration* (1887). This 'common good' has a number of different dimensions, in both civil society and in government. It covers volunteering, civic participation, a sense of public duty and public employment. It is this latter aspect of public service that is the focus of this book. It is the idea that public servants will put aside their own interests, motivated by a sense of public service or public duty, and that this is a 'higher order' of commitment than to self, tribe or family (Horton, 2008).

But by the middle of the 20th century, the idea that public employees were working in the public interest was increasingly under attack. A wave of academics and others started to question what the 'public interest' really meant, how it was operationalised and whether other interests might be at play.

These views started to influence politicians, particularly with the election of Margaret Thatcher in the UK in 1979 (Le Grand, 2003) and Ronald Reagan in the USA in 1980. But it did not take long for public interest fightback to begin. This started with the publication of a highly cited and influential article 'The motivational bases of public service' by James Perry and Lois Wise (1990). In this article, the authors asserted that public service motivation is an individual's 'predisposition to respond to motives grounded primarily or uniquely in public institutions or organisations' (p 368) and included 'a desire to serve the public interest' (p 370). Their conception of, and empirical evidence for, public service motivation has since developed to become almost hegemonic in the academic field of public administration, and has considerable real-world impact on the design and delivery of public services.

This book aims to critically evaluate public service motivation, both its theory and the empirical evidence supporting it. In doing so, I do not question that some people may act altruistically, or that individuals might be motivated by being seen to contribute to the public good. But there are significant issues with PSMT as it is currently conceived, its explanation of how public employees perceive and further the public interest, and substantive gaps in how it considers public servants' collective decision-making. Ignoring these issues and gaps, and designing public decision-making, public services and public employment practices around assumptions based on the idea that politicians and public employees are motivated by, and make decisions in, the public interest, raises the prospect of serious misalignment of the state.

My focus in this book is on public employees, what motivates public employees in their work and whether PSMT provides a comprehensive and convincing explanation of public employees' work motivation. I recognise that many within the field argue that public service motivation explains other regarding motives in all settings, job roles and circumstances. Yet despite these assertions, the most commonly used definition of public service motivation roots it in public organisations (O'Leary, 2019), and most empirical research is focused on public employees (Ritz et al, 2016). (Perhaps because, as Gene Brewer explains, the public sector provides greater opportunities to serve the public (Brewer, 2019).)

There are two further reasons I focus on public employees. The first is the uniqueness of government as an employer. It is outwith the scope of this book to engage in a lengthy debate as to the uniqueness or otherwise of public organisations and public management compared to other forms of organisations. There is a huge literature on this debate (Pollitt, 2016), to which I could not hope to make a meaningful contribution here. I recognise that it is a debate within the PSMT literature, with some stating that public employment is different. For example, James Perry has stated that: 'Conventional wisdom and empirical evidence that public employees are different led Perry and Wise (1990) to define a construct, public service motivation (PSM), intended to capture the distinction' (Perry, 1997: 182). Whereas Gene A Brewer comments that: 'the suggestion that government employees are different from ordinary citizens runs counter to mainstream public administration theory and popular thought' (Brewer, 2019: 213).

In this, I agree with Gene Brewer. Government employees are also ordinary citizens. They are no different to ordinary citizens except that they are public employees. It is the distinctiveness of government as an employer that makes the difference: because of the non-market and monopolistic nature of government work, because of the role played by politicians and public policy in government and because of the central role played by furthering the public interest generates different incentives and constraints on the actions of public employees compared to other sectors. This distinctiveness provides institutional incentives and constraints on the behaviours of those who work in the public sector. It also affects, and is affected by, the preferences or motives of those employees, particularly in terms of furthering the public interest. It is for this reason that my focus here is on public employees.

The second, and controversial, reason for focusing on public employees is that I would argue that the other regarding actions of public employees as they go about their everyday work are not the same as seemingly similar actions by ordinary citizens in everyday life. To illustrate this difference, compare the motives of a passer-by who runs into a burning building to save the child of someone unknown to them, and the motives of a professional firefighter who takes the same action. The passer-by is plausibly motivated by what Andreoni (1990) calls 'pure' altruism. The firefighter might also be so motivated. But she also gets paid for her job. Her job is one that is (quite rightly) held in very high esteem and valued greatly by others. Being a firefighter is an important part of her identity. This esteem and positive reinforcement of her identity both provide benefits to the firefighter, and as such is not the same as the 'pure' altruism behind the passer-by's actions.

Expressively motivated public employees

I believe there is an alternative explanation of what is being observed in the PSMT empirical literature. In the second part of the book, I set out this alternative. It is that public employees are expressively motivated in their work.

This explanation is rooted in rationalism. It starts with a rejection of the idea that rationalism means only selfish motives and behaviours. Rather, it is assumed that a rational public servant's utility function incorporates a range of goals, self-regarding and other regarding, instrumental *and expressive*. This assumption is not novel. Economists have always assumed that an individual's utility function was wider than instrumental self-interest. Since the 1960s, there has been growing theoretical and empirical research rooted in the idea that self-regarding and other regarding motives are consistent with rationality. This is part of a wider development in rational choice theory, that has seen substantive work around rational ignorance (Downs, 1997 [1957]; Somin, 1998), rational irrationality (Caplan, 2001) and expressive choice. It is this latter development – expressive motivation – that provides the framework for the second half of this book.

Expressive motivation is about intrinsic motivation (Chong, 2000; Hillman, 2010). It is about deriving benefit from the action itself, not from the outcome of that action. For public employees, I argue that the action of working for the public sector provides an important intrinsic motivation.

But it can also be about values, and about identity. Expressive behaviour is action that enables a rational actor to confirm to herself and to others important aspects of her identity and the values that are important to her. A rational actor might be motivated to express her values and beliefs, and take action that enables her to do so. She might be motivated by the desire to demonstrate her positive, prosocial attributes of being generous, cooperative, trusting, and her moral values. In doing so, the rational actor might be motivated by self-approval, but also the approval of others.

This expressive account has not previously been used to explain the motivations of public employees. Expressive rationality is most often used to explain voting behaviour, which is where most of the theoretical and empirical research is focused. However, expressive rationality has also been used to explain consumer boycotts (Tyran and Engelmann, 2005), strike action (Brunnschweiler et al, 2014) and a number of other political behaviours. It provides a very different explanation of the motives of public employees, with very different behavioural consequences, to that outlined in PSMT. Like much of PSMT, this expressive account starts from the basis that intrinsic motivation is an important energiser for working in the public sector. It also sees serving the public interest as being core to the motivation of public sector employees. But this is not a higher-order, other regarding motivation. Rather, being seen to work in the public interest provides expressive utility to the individual public employee. She gains utility both from confirming to herself her public interested identity, but also from others around her confirming this identify.

In this expressive account, the expressively motivated public employee is indifferent to whether she actually furthers the public interest. She does not need to have definition of the public interest, or have some conception of what might and what might not be in the public interest, or know whether public policies, programmes and public services really do further the public interest. Because what is important is the role that furthering the public interest plays in her sense of identity, and the expressive utility she derives from confirming this identity.

This explanation is likely to be controversial and at this stage, it is only a theory. But for me it has the potential to better explain observed public sector outcomes, and also directly addresses significant gaps in PSMT. I set out the basis for this explanation, and some of the potential consequences for our understanding of public administration, in the second half of this book. But before I do so, I want to critically evaluate PSMT. I start here by exploring how the theory came to be developed.

Background: self-interest and public employees

To understand the birth of PSMT, it is important to understand the context within which it developed. This shaped the early development of PSMT and, for me, explains some of its current gaps and limitations. For PSMT can be seen as a reaction to two major developments in public administration in the second half of the 20th century: the Public Choice revolution, and New Public Management, and an attempt to reassert an older theory, that of the public service ethos.

The Public Choice revolution

Most public policy or public administration programmes today do not explicitly cover Public Choice, and few public administration academics research or write from a Public Choice perspective. So it would be easy to underestimate the profound effect that Public Choice had on theoretical and empirical understandings of government, and on politics more generally.

Starting in the 1940s and 1950s with the works of Kenneth Arrow, Duncan Black and Anthony Downs, the Public Choice revolution really took hold from the mid-1960s with the works of Mancur Olson, Gordon Tullock, James Buchanan, Elinor Ostrom, Anne Krueger and William Niskanen. Public choice is often described as being the application of economics to the study of politics (Shughart and Razzolini, 2001). It is the study of government behaviour or, more accurately, the study of the collective behaviour of individuals within government (Tullock et al, 2005). Its focus is on collective, non-market decisions, and how these are affected by, and effect, the institutional design of government. Core to Public Choice, and particularly to understanding how Public Choice influenced the early development of PSMT, are three fundamental assumptions. First, that humans are rational actors, our actions are reasoned and have consequences. Flowing from the assumption of rationality, we are rational in all contexts, whether we are engaged in collective or individual decisions, whether we vote or buy goods from a supermarket, whether we work in the private or public sector (in the Public Choice literature, this is known as the *symmetry assumption*).

Second, our rational decisions are influenced by the institutional context around us. This is particularly important because of the unique institutional arrangements of government, especially its monopolistic, non-market and collective nature. Government is inherently a monopoly. No jurisdiction can have more than one president or prime minister, and there cannot be more than one legislative body governing any given area of law. Government can of course create monopolies, grant monopolistic power to a private organisation, or allow monopolists to exploit their monopolistic position.

Government is also inherently a collective endeavour. The goods and services provided by government are collective in nature, and generally have some social outcome over and above the benefit they generate for individual recipients.

Third, that as rational actors, public employees and politicians face the same information problems, the same collective action problems, and the same *fundamental uncertainty* as everyone else (see, for example, Dow, 2015). As such, public servants are not omnipotent or omniscient, and government failure is as likely as market failure.

It is clear that the early development of PSMT was in response to the Public Choice movement, and to its effect on the organisation and delivery of public services. Perry and Wise (1990) state this in their seminal article, and this point is repeated in a number of important articles and books on public service motivation. Perry and Wise asserted that Public Choice 'called into question' the strength of the public service ethic, and that it 'stands in opposition to the view that public service motives energise and direct the behavior [*sic*] of civil servants' (p 368). They identify the rationality assumptions of Public Choice as the key driver of this. I will address these assumptions (and how a narrow understanding of these assumptions directly affected the early development of PSMT) later in this chapter. However, it is the third assumption – that government failure is as likely as market failure – that for me had a profound effect on my early work on PSMT.

Despite its claims to be a scientific, positivist analysis of government (Tullock et al, 2005), there is a significant normative bent to much of Public Choice. Much of this normative side of Public Choice is focused on the structure and organisation of government, and ways of minimising the risk of government failure. Competition between parts of government bureaucracy; limiting the size and scope of the state; constitutional arrangements that favour checks and balances, and focuses on localised decision-making, all feature in the normative aspects of Public Choice, and all were profoundly influential in governance and policy in the 1970s and 1980s. The canon of Public Choice works is extensive and goes far beyond the motivations of public sector employees. But there are three works that are particularly relevant, both to understanding how Public Choice scholars conceive bureaucracy, and the position against which PSMT was founded. These three works are Anthony Downs' *Inside bureaucracy* (1967), William Niskanen's *Bureaucracy and representative government* (1971), and Patrick Dunleavy's *Democracy, bureaucracy and public choice* (1991).

Inside bureaucracy is not specifically about government bureaucracy, but bureaucracy in general and in all forms. Echoing earlier work by Ludwig von Mises (Niskanen, 2001), Downs defined bureaucracy to cover any organisation or part of an organisation not directly involved in market transactions. And while much of this work examines the life cycle and behaviour of bureaucratic organisations, it is Downs' assumptions about the motivations and behaviours of individual bureaucrats that are of relevance to the argument set out here. Downs starts by recognising that the term bureaucrat is generally used derogatively, and thereafter instead uses the term 'official'. He makes clear that officials are rational individuals, and that they have a complex set of goals that they are seeking to achieve. These include: 'power, income, prestige, security ... pride in excellent work, *and desire to serve the public interest* (as the individual official conceives it)' (Downs, 1967, emphasis added). Downs then goes on to identify two types of 'purely self-interested' officials: 'climbers', who he suggests are motivated by power, prestige and income; and 'conservers' who seek to maximise their security, maintaining their status and employment benefits.

Downs goes on to identify three groups of bureaucrats who have *mixed motives,* whose motives 'combine self-interest and altruistic loyalty to larger values'. His three groups – zealots, advocates and statesperson are focused on differing levels of policy and organisational loyalty, and each 'seek power and prestige for personal as well as altruistic reasons'. And, importantly, this is not the only time that Downs goes beyond self-interest to explain the actions of rational actors. In his *Economic theory of democracy* (1957), Downs makes it clear that political behaviour may be driven by concern for the welfare of others.

It is William Niskanen's work, which is more directly focused on the motives and behaviours of public employees, that was more influential on the early development of PSMT. Its influence on Public Choice theory and empirical work, and real-world decisions about the scope and structure of government bureaucracies, was significant. Niskanen makes two arguments about the behaviour of public employees, and specifically senior bureaucrats. Both arguments flow from Niskanen's assumption that public employees are rational individuals, with interests that are separate from, and sometimes different to, the interests of the governments they serve or to the public interest. First, he argues that the relationship between government bureaucracy and governments (politicians, members of governments) is a bilateral monopoly. The bureaucracy provides policy advice and is the only provider of this advice; and governments are their only consumers.

Second, Niskanen argues that the relationship suffers from principal-agent problems. Politicians are unable to hold civil servants to account because of lack of time, information and understanding (Cope, 2000). Indeed, this principal-agent problem is exacerbated because there is no market value to the work of the bureaucracy (Downs, 1967). Because of this, bureaucrats will oversupply policy advice and public services (Matthewson, 1996). They do so to maximise the size of their budgets, which allows them to further their interests in terms of salary, reputation, power and patronage (Blais and Dion, 1990).

It is these two Public Choice assumptions – that bureaucrats are rational and motivated by self-interest, and that this might lead to outcomes that are not in the public interest – that had a significant influence on the development of PSMT.

For both challenge the assumption of government, and government employees, working for the higher purpose of the public interest.

But even before Perry and Wise put forward public service motivation as an alternative explanation of public employees' motives, Niskanen's budget-maximisation theory was being heavily criticised. Indeed, in 1985 Patrick Dunleavy set out a different Public Choice model of public employee behaviour, his *bureau-shaping* model, which he later further developed in his 1991 book, *Democracy, bureaucracy and public choice: economic explanations in political science* (Dunleavy, 1991). Although Dunleavy posited the bureau-shaping model as a criticism of Niskanen, I would argue it complements and further develops the budget maximising model.

Like Niskanen, Dunleavy starts with an assumption that public employees are rational, and have their own interests. He then sets out to augment the types of interest that rational public employees might seek to further, adding closeness to policy and power, avoiding routine management and operational responsibilities, and having high levels of discretion. Dunleavy argues that public employees might engage in collective action rather than individual action to further their interests. Whether, and to what extent, this action is focused on budget maximisation is influenced by differences in agency form and function, and in budget composition. These differences will incentivise and constrain the extent to which public employees engage in budget maximisation or bureau-shaping strategies. These differences root the bureau-shaping thesis in *rational choice institutionalism*; that human action is incentivised and constrained by the institutional setting in which decisions are made, and that human action affects the institutional 'rules of the game' that we face as rational actors.

Dunleavy identifies five basic types of government agency: (a) delivery agencies; (b) transfer agencies, which handle transfer payments (benefits, for example) from government to citizens or firms; (c) contract agencies, which manage research and development, building or service contracts; (d) control agencies, which manage funding grants to other government agencies and parts of the public sector; and (e) regulatory agencies (Dunleavy, 1991). These different agency types will vary in terms of the composition of their budgets. He identifies four budget types, arguing that different agency types will have a different 'mix' of these four. Dunleavy argues that civil servants' behaviour will be influenced by, first, whether bureaucrats can further their interests individually or collectively, and second, the type of agency and budget mix. This might be to pursue budget maximising behaviour, or rather to 'shape' the size and scope of their agencies to further their interests.

The bureau–shaping model initially generated much needed theoretical debate (Shaw, 2004), but to date empirical testing of the model has been limited. Much of the existing empirical work is focused on the UK (James, 2003; Gains and John, 2010; O'Leary, 2015; Ribbins and Sherratt, 2015), with studies also in Australia (Dollery and Hamburger, 1996), New Zealand (Shaw, 2004), China (Fan, 2015), Taiwan (Kuo, 2012), France and the USA (Matthewson, 1996). Most studies have focused on aggregate changes in budgets, and few on the motivations of public employees. (A notable exception is the work of Francesca Gains and Peter John (2010) around local government employees, and my previous research (2015)).

Dunleavy's bureau–shaping thesis is important here in three ways. First, because *Democracy, bureaucracy, and public choice* was published at around the same time as the Perry and Wise article. Yet while theoretical interest and empirical research around PSMT has grown each year since, interest in the bureau–shaping model has dwindled, with nothing published since 2015. Second, the thesis is important because it recognises public employees might pursue collective action when individual action is unsuccessful. Finally, Dunleavy recognises that interest in public policy is a rational self-interest for many undertaking government work, an assumption his model shares with some within the field of public service motivation. Yet, despite these similarities, Dunleavy's work hardly appears in the PSMT literature, as I shall discuss in Chapter Four.

New Public Management

As Perry and Wise were drafting their article, another public administration scholar, Christopher Hood, was setting out his analysis of profound changes in the organisation and delivery of public administration in the UK and elsewhere. He first did so in his inaugural lecture at the London School of Economics, and subsequently in more detail in another seminal and often cited article, 'A public management for all seasons?' (Hood, 1991). In this article, he categorised a series of public administration and public management reforms that had taken place in the 1970s and 1980s under the term New Public Management (NPM). NPM is often described as being about the '3 Ms' of markets, management and measurement (Ferlie, 2017), or alternatively as disaggregation, competition and incentivisation (Dunleavy et al, 2006). It is the adoption and use of management practices associated with the private sector into public administration and public services (Dunleavy and Hood, 1994).

Christopher Hood directly linked these NPM developments to Public Choice, and specifically to 'Niskanen's (1971) landmark theory of bureaucracy and the spate of later work which built on it' (p 5). Hood is not alone in making this link. Belle and Ongaro (2014), Van de Walle and Hammerschmid (2011) and Boruvka and Perry (2020) also make this connection, as do several Public Choice scholars. Hood identified four 'megatrends' and seven 'doctrinal components' of NPM, of which the latter is interesting here. Of the seven, three explicitly relate to normative Public Choice ideas. Hood's fourth and fifth doctrines are a 'shift to disaggregation of units in the public sector' and 'shift to greater competition in the public sector'. Both of these doctrines also appear as founding themes in Dunleavy and colleagues' (2006) analysis, and both talk directly to Niskanen's concerns about bureaucratic monopolies within government. They also talk to wider normative propositions from the field around the need for greater competition between government bureau and parts of government.

NPM is a broad and contested concept. It has been applied to a number of public administration reforms since the 1980s, even if the reforms do not fit the all-encompassing definitions of NPM. It is not particularly well-defined or coherent. Despite this lack of clarity, NPM research has been core to public administration, political science and other social science disciplines since the publication of Christopher Hood's seminal paper. Indeed, over the 30-year period to 2020, some 500 articles have been published that include 'New Public Management' in the title, compared to around 350 with 'Public Service Motivation', although the pace of publication for the latter is increasing. As such, NPM and PSMT rank as the two largest areas of contemporary public administration research.

It is worth highlighting that there are significant differences between the NPM and PSMT research agendas. Whereas almost all of the PSMT literature provides a positive view of public service motivation and of the practice of public administration (Brewer, 2019), most of the NPM literature is critical in nature. PSMT mainly focuses on empirical (and particularly quantitative) research; the NPM literature is largely theoretical in nature, often linking these reforms to other concepts such as 'neoliberalism'. When NPM research is empirical, it generally uses qualitative methods. And, finally, the NPM literature focuses on government, on the relationship between citizens and the state, and on public management approaches (Van de Walle and Hammerschmid, 2011). In contrast, PSMT focuses on public employees.

The argument here is that Public Choice Theory and NPM influenced the early development of PSMT in three, possibly four, ways.

It is worth highlighting the quite different political positions sometimes associated with academics working in the fields of Public Choice and PSMT. Public Choice is often accused of having a right-wing bias, because of its normative focus on smaller government, and particularly its promotion of competition as a means of driving efficiency. In contrast, PSMT is more left leaning, with several authors suggesting that left wing politics is an antecedent of public service motivation. James Perry, for example, argues that political ideology is an important antecedent of public service motivation. He identifies that American political parties have historically taken different positions on the size and role of the state, perhaps implying that small state and low tax views are not consistent with public service motivation. He goes on to state that: 'Political beliefs should bear on an individual's public service motivation. A direct measure of political beliefs is conservatism/liberalism. Increasing liberalism should be positively related to public service motivation' (Perry, 1997: 186).

This assertion is echoed in Mark Prebble's critical account of public service motivation (Prebble, 2016). Prebble suggests that the constructs used to measure public service motivation include a number of dimensions that are potentially politically biased, and omit dimensions often associated with more conservative ideological views. While there is no evidence to suggest that these differences were significant in the development of PSMT, I would argue that some of the PSMT literature appears to equate the public interest with more government and more government spending, and implies (as James Perry has) that left leaning public servants will have higher levels of public service motivation.

Regardless of whether the development of PSMT was a reaction to the politics underlying Public Choice and NPM, there are three significant ways in which they did and continue to affect PSMT. First, some attribute the malaise in public administration and growing distrust in government in the 1980s and 1990s to the NPM reforms. This line of argument suggests that the NPM reforms changed the values of the public sector, affected the ethics of public employees, generated a focus on extrinsic (specifically, pecuniary) rewards, and led to the importation of private sector managers and management techniques. This clash of values and management techniques – between the new approaches that focused on performance, efficiency, lower costs, and more responsiveness to service users and the tradition that focused on 'equity, professionalism, public interest, procedural safeguards, acceptance of superordination and subordination, impartiality, and neutrality' (Meyer et al, 2014: 865), and this demotivated public servants. These reforms were characterised as being 'strong on organizing, but weak on the public good' (Noordegraaf and van Bockel, 2006: 585).

Setting aside for a moment the difficulty of seeing more efficient and lower-cost public services as somehow *not* being in the public interest, this line of argument does not really stack up. Many of the individual reforms now labelled as NPM were proposed because of an existing crisis of confidence in government. So, for example, in *Reinventing government*, one of the canonical texts proposing reforms now known as NPM, David Osborne and Ted Gaebler (1992) state that 'cynicism about government runs deep' and that 'governments are in deep trouble today'. They go on to say that their book: 'is for those who care about government – because they work in government, or work with government, or study government, or simply want their governments to be more effective. It is for those who know something is wrong, but are not sure just how to what it is' (Osborne and Gaebler, 1992: xv).

So while NPM reforms might well have deepened this crisis, they could not have been the cause. This is certainly recognised in some of the PSMT literature – Perry and Wise, for example, state that this malaise began in the mid-1960s, sometime before any of the reforms now labelled as NPM were implemented. And there is no empirical evidence that measures changes in levels of public employees' motivation during the period of these reforms, so it is impossible to know whether these reforms affected the motivation and performance of public employees. But despite this, PSMT offered a solution to the ills generated by NPM, by 'management policies and practices with greater fidelity both to human behavior [*sic*] and to fit with values like the public interest and common good embodied in public institutions' (Boruvka and Perry, 2020: 566).

Second, both Public Choice and NPM raised questions about the motivations of public employees that challenged the status quo *public service ethos* assumption. Public Choice explicitly, and NPM implicitly, start from a position that human beings make reasoned and self-interested decisions *regardless of setting*. That we do not fundamentally become different people in different contexts or situations, that public employees have the same motivations as everyone else (this is an assumption of symmetry in Public Choice). Coupled with narratives about the need to reform government and public administration, of a bloated, inefficient and unresponsive public sector, Public Choice and NPM questioned the uniqueness and 'higher calling' of public service, and much of normative public administration research.

Third, PSMT misconstrued and continues to misrepresent the understanding of rationality inherent to Public Choice (Prebble, 2016; O'Leary, 2019). Many definitions of public service motivation state that it is other regarding, and that this is the opposite of self-interested motivation. And these definitions conceive rationality as being only about self-interest (Perry and Hondeghem, 2008: 8), and that this self-interest is selfish, about extrinsic reward and about 'personal gain' (Wise, 2004: 673). They also assume that Public Choice theory cannot explain other regarding behaviours, and that it 'deride(s) collective action and normatively promote individual initiative as overwhelmingly superior to collective action' (Koehler and Rainey, 2008: 50).

As both Mark Prebble (2016) and I (2015; 2019) have previously argued, there are a number of problems with this depiction of rational choice theory generally, and of Public Choice in particular. It is important to first understand that there is no such thing as rational choice *theory*; rather, it is an umbrella term to describe different ways of conceiving human rational choices, with at least 30 variants representing different fields within rational choice (Herne and Setala, 2004). And, rational choice is just one of a family of rationality models (Ostrom, 1998). In particular, the concept of bounded rationality (Simon, 1947), which assumes that humans aim to be rational, but are unable to be because of cognitive limits, imperfect information and fundamental uncertainty. And while Public Choice might be considered to be a branch of rational choice theory, it has developed its own understanding of human collective, political behaviour.

One problem with how PSMT understands Public Choice is the conflation of rationality with selfish self-interest. This makes two mistakes. First, it confuses rationality as the formal structure of human agency with the decision content of that structure. The structure of human behaviour – that we have preferences/goals, that we considered the options available to us to achieve these goals and that we, subject to incentives and constraints, choose the option that is best able to achieve our goals – makes no assumptions about what individual actor's preferences might be, which options she considers, and how she accounts for different incentives and constraints.

Second, PSMT assumes that rationality means self-interested, and that self-interested equates to selfish. But neither of these assumptions are actually consistent with the core premise of Public Choice theory.

Take, for example, the motivational assumptions of William Niskanen and Anthony Downs. Both authors are cited in PSMT works as asserting that public employees are rational and self-interested. But both made clear in their writings that public servants might be motivated by a whole range of different goals, including serving the public interest. William Niskanen, for example, states that 'the output of the bureau' is of the possible goals of a rational public servant. He goes on to say: 'Some bureaucrats, either by predisposition or indoctrination, undoubtedly try to serve (their perception) of the public interest' (Niskanen, 1971: 39). The output of the bureau here means advice to government ministers, public policy and of course public services. Indeed, of the eight potential preferences or goals that Niskanen identifies with public servants' utility function, only one is selfish and pecuniary in nature.

Equally, Anthony Downs (1967) makes clear that bureaucrats might have mixed motives, a range of different goals they might seek to achieve. He states that public servants seek to obtain their goals rationally, by which he means 'in the most efficient manner' (p 4), and provides eight examples of what these goals might be. These include: 'loyalty (to an idea, an institution, or the nation), pride in excellent work, and desire to serve the public interest (as the individual official conceives of it)' (p 4).

Indeed, Herbert Simon – whose critique of rational choice theory was core to his bounded rationality thesis – observed that 'rationality is orthogonal to selfishness'. He then stated that rational goals might include:

> the possession of wealth, the consumption of wealth, the amassing of power, the accumulation of the good will of other people, the acquisition of glory. ... If we define an altruist as someone whose utility lies in giving pleasure to other people, altruism is entirely compatible with the economist's definition of utility. (Simon, 1995: 48)

Andrew Hindmoor, in his 2006 book *Rational choice*, states that rational actors might pursue goals that might be self-regarding, other regarding, or a mixture of the two. He makes clear that 'rationality does *not* imply egotism' (p 2, emphasis in original). William Riker (1990) has explained that, while rational actors are assumed to be self-interested, rationalists make no assumptions about the content of that self-interest; it may be egotistical and it may be altruistic. As such, self-interest is simply what provides the most satisfaction.

So why does PSMT make a link between rationality and self-interest? To be fair, this is a link often made within the Public Choice literature. Several canonical texts refer to self-interest as a core assumption of rationality. And they are not alone in criticising Public Choice about its focus on self-interest. But the challenge for both those within and without PSMT is that this narrow definition of rationality is increasingly rejected by those within rational choice theory. It is being replaced by a wider, more inclusive conception of rationality, so that 'a significant number of economists have now abandoned it and at least six (of whom) … (Frederick Hayek, Gunnar Myrdal, Herbert Simon, Ronald Coase, Amartya Sen and Daniel Kahneman) have been awarded Nobel prizes' (Hodgson, 2012, as cited in O'Leary, 2019: 94).

Conclusion

PSMT developed in response to a series of reforms instigated under what is now referred to as New Public Management, and a view of human rationality and of government promoted by Public Choice theory. This response – generated at first from within the academic field of public administration – was to reassert the concept of the public service ethos, and to formalise this as an explanation of what motivates public employees. This ethos, which entails a commitment to public service and to furthering the public interest, is an old and enduring idea. It is an ideal, a series of expectations of public servants, encapsulated in the UK in the Victorian establishment of the permanent civil service following the Northcote-Trevelyn report of 1854. This proposed a civil service appointed through merit and through open competition, and with core values of integrity, honesty, objectivity and impartiality. In particular, civil servants were expected to put the obligations of public service above their own personal interests, to further the public interest.

It is these values that PSMT seeks both to theorise formally, to empirically evidence, but also further normatively. Their key thesis is that public servants are motivated by serving the public interest, by the meaningfulness of their work and its contribution to this public interest. Despite the significant growth in research on public service motivation over the past 30 years, this thesis – the empirical evidence used to support it, and the conclusions drawn from it about the recruitment and retention of public employees – have hardly been subjected to much critical evaluation.

The purpose of this book is to do just that, and to provide an alternative explanation of the motives and behaviours of public employees.

The book is structured as follows. The first part of the book covers Chapters Two, Three, Four and Five and are focused on critiquing PSMT. In the following chapter, I explore how public service motivation is defined and conceptualised. This is not an easy task, both because its theoretical underpinnings have changed considerably over the past 30 years, and because there is still huge debate in the field about what exactly public service motivation is, and whether and how it is different to others within the family of other regarding motives and behaviours.

In Chapter Three, the concept of the public interest is examined, as this plays a pivotal role in PSMT. Questions are posed about what this means, how it is understood and what it means for public servants' behaviours. The fundamental question asked is this: if the public plays such a fundamental role in PSMT, why is there no discussion or explanation as to how public service motivated civil servants might discern the public will or what constitutes the public interest? This leads to the discussion in Chapter Four about decision-making within PSMT. Given the assertion by many PSMT scholars that motivation affects behaviour, I explore how public service motivated civil servants make decisions, both individually and collectively. In the final chapter examining PSMT, the empirical evidence used to evidence the existence and effect of public service motivation is examined and evaluated.

The second part of the book consists of two chapters. In Chapter Six, an alternative explanation of observed public service motivation is provided. I argue that rather than being the opposite to rationality, what is being observed and theorised is entirely consistent with rational choice theory. In my final chapter, I draw a series of conclusions about what this means for our study of public administration.

PART I

A critique of public service motivation theory

TWO

Conceptualising public service motivation

Introduction

In the 30 years since Perry and Wise (1990) first formalised public service motivation, it has become a dominant concept in public administration. Theoretical and empirical research has grown significantly, with hundreds of articles being published in each of the last few years. Indeed, Gene A Brewer recently suggested that public service motivation research has become a cottage industry, and is one of the 'hottest topics' in public administration research (Brewer, 2019).

This puts public administration scholarship at odds with wider political science, where rational choice theory has been described as being the dominant paradigm. More importantly, the near hegemonic status of public service motivation in the public administration scholarship raises significant questions about how the concept is defined and understood. Some of these questions have been raised elsewhere, from both within and outside the PSMT community. In this chapter, I explore how the concept has developed over the past 30 years, and some of the current fault lines in how it is understood. In doing so, I argue that it is not a coherent concept; it is not clearly differentiated from other similar ideas, and there are still significant areas of debate around the scope of public service motivation. I am not the first to make such arguments, nor am I alone in arguing that more theoretical work needs to be done before we can hope to understand what the empirical results really mean. But there are several areas of this debate to which this book hopefully contributes.

Public service motivation theory as a middle-range theory

PSMT is not intended to be a complete theory of human social action. It is a middle-range theory, intended to provide specific and testable hypotheses, linking empirical evidence and theory building in practical ways in relation to specific situations or contexts. Indeed, this is one of the undoubted strengths of PSMT. Rather than focusing on endless grand, or post hoc theorising (Green and Shapiro, 1995), PSMT provides concrete and real propositions that could and should make a real-world difference.

PSMT is focused on predispositions and motivations of individuals engaging in public institutions. As a middle-range theory, it is not intended to provide a grand theory of publicness, the public interest, public policy, or of public administration. PSMT is a middle-range theory, and as such can contribute to public administration scholarship in a number of important ways (Abner et al, 2017).

But such approaches can and should be linked to other middle-range theories, and should not start with assumptions that are outwith more general understandings of our social reality. PSMT needs to work alongside, complement and be consistent with our broader understanding of government and public administration. It needs to interact with models that explain how collective decisions are made about which public policy programmes to implement, maintain, or terminate. It needs to be consistent with our understanding of the policy making process. It needs to talk to models of bureaucratic politics and executive politics. So far, PSMT does not seem to do so in any coherent or convincing manner. Indeed, as many of these other theories are rooted in rational choice, it is unlikely that it could.

The Perry and Wise (1990) definition of public service motivation

The most commonly used definition of public service motivation is that it is a 'predisposition to respond to motives grounded primarily or uniquely in public institutions and organisations' (Perry and Wise, 1990: 368). This definition is core to much of the theoretical and empirical PSMT work. It is used or referred to in most published works on public service motivation, and is given as the formal definition of the concept in James Perry's most recent book, *Managing organizations to sustain passion for public service* (Perry, 2021). Motivation here is 'the forces that energize, direct, and sustain behavior [*sic*]' (Perry and Porter, 1982). This motivation is seen to be purposeful, and goal-orientated; indeed, James Perry (2021) makes clear that PSMT draws on Edwin Locke and Gary Latham's (1990) goal theory, which links motivation, goals and values to individual behaviour and performance.

Perry and Wise (1990) also drew heavily from David Knoke and Christine Wright-Isak's (1982) predisposition-opportunity theory, which suggests that individuals act on three types of social motives. These three dimensions – rational, normative, affective – play a fundamental and often controversial role in PSMT. Rational motives are ground in utility maximisation, and thereby draw directly on economics and rational choice theory-based understanding of goal-orientated human behaviour. (Indeed, it is this dimension which has proved to be the most controversial aspect and one which is hotly debated within PSMT scholarship, as discussed in Chapter Four.) Perry and Wise associated rational motives with an attraction to public policy making. They and others (for example, Adrian Ritz (2011)) have argued that policy making is a feature that is unique to government work, and is likely to be a motivator for many people entering public service.

Normative motives are actions based on a desire to follow norms. These motives are associated with a commitment to the public interest, which Perry and Wise (1990) argue is core to most discussions of the foundations of public service. Indeed, as discussed in Chapter Three, the public interest is fundamental to much work on public service motivation. Affective motives are behaviours that are grounded in emotional responses to social situations. They drive compassion for others, and actions rooted in self-sacrifice. Each of these different motivational drivers are other regarding (Perry and Hondeghem, 2008), about wanting to help and work for others rather than self. This identification of public service motivation with other regarding behaviours is core to PSMT.

A core idea of predisposition-opportunity theory, and one that features heavily in PSMT, is the idea the individuals' organisational commitment and positive work action depends on there being a match between their individual motivations and the organisational incentive structure. Much of the PSMT literature draws on attraction-selection-attrition theory (Schneider et al, 1995), person-organisation fit and person-environment fit theories as ways of exploring this matching process. These are often discussed in relation to recruitment and selection in the public sector, drawing on a core assumption underlying much of PSMT that the 'characteristics of the public sector employee and work environment are different from the private sector' (Leisink and Steijn, 2008: 121).

Finally, and core to the discussion here, PSMT draws on self-determination theory (Deci and Ryan, 1985). This is a theory of motivation that examines how our social situation and context might 'facilitate versus forestall the natural processes of self-motivation and healthy psychological development' (Ryan and Deci, 2000: 68). There are a number of components to this theory, but four are important here. First, as with the definition of motivation by Perry and Porter (1982), this theory sees motivation as being connected to behaviour, and as such has consequences. Second, Deci and Ryan identify three innate psychological needs that all humans share; competence, relatedness and autonomy. They argue that levels of motivation are related to the extent that these three psychological needs are met. Third, they identify a continuum of different motives, ranging from external regulation through to intrinsic motivation. It is this concept of intrinsic motivation that is core to my discussion later in this chapter, as it raises a serious inconsistency in PSMT. Fourth, both self-determination theory and predisposition-opportunity theory provide insight into how individuals and organisations interact, and thereby provide the institutional content for PSMT (Vandenabeele, 2007; Corduneanu et al, 2020; Vogel, 2020).

A concept with many definitions

Although the Perry and Wise definition of public service motivation is the most commonly cited, it is by far not the only way in which this form of motivation is conceived. There is a plethora of different definitions, emphasising different aspects of public service motivation. Bozeman and Su (2015) identify over 20 different definitions, with several key authors providing different conceptions over the past 30 years. Mark Prebble, in an article in the *American Review of Public Administration*, identified eight different definitions, and found that the Perry and Wise conception was the most commonly used (Prebble, 2016). There are several definitions offered by different authors in the edited book by Perry and Hondeghem (2008), and several articles reference differing conceptions.

There are many key lines of difference between these definitions. Some relate public service motivation with altruism (Rainey and Steinbauer, 1999; Bright, 2008; Perry and Hondeghem, 2008; Alcoba and Phinaitrup, 2020), though the relationship between these two concepts has been 'nebulous' (Bozeman and Su, 2015) and continues to be contested (Jensen and Andersen, 2015; Schott et al, 2019). Others relate it to prosocial motivation or prosocial behaviour (Perry and

Hondeghem, 2008; Kim and Vandenabeele, 2010), though there is debate about what prosocial motivation means and how prosociability is reflected in the different domains of public service motivation (Schott et al, 2019; Awan et al, 2020). Some suggest that public service motivation is distinct from prosocial motivation (Corduneanu et al, 2020).

In the last few years, there have been several attempts to clarify some of these conceptual inconsistencies and gaps. But despite these attempts, public service motivation continues to lack conceptual clarity and distinctiveness. And, as argued in Chapter Five, empirical work compounds this, making it even less clear what public service motivation *actually* is, and how it is distinct from fellow other regarding motivators and behaviours.

Public sector or societal?

There is one aspect of public service motivation that is fundamental to the Perry and Wise definition that has also proved to be one of the more contested areas in PSMT. It is that public service motivation is rooted in public organisations and institutions and is therefore about employment in the public sector. This controversy has a number of dimensions, and goes to the heart of the debate about whether public service motivation is a distinct and useful concept.

Much PSMT focuses on the 'public' aspect of public service motivation as being in relation to government, and contrasts this with work in the private sector. James Perry (2021) and Sylvia Horton (2008) are among many authors who locate the origins of PSMT in the concept of public service ethic, in 'the call of public service', 'that what motivates public servants goes beyond the factors that motivate others in the private sector' (Perry, 2021: 20).

In a systematic review of the PSMT literature, Adrian Ritz, Gene Brewer and Oliver Neumann (2016) make clear that public service motivation is mostly used to explain other regarding motivations in public employees. Sangmook Kim, who developed two instruments for measuring public service motivation, states that 'PSM pertains to government employees' (Kim, 2009: 151), a theme that is repeated in much of the literature. Many authors make the argument that individuals with higher levels of public service motivation are more likely to seek public sector employment, and to perform better in public sector jobs (see, for example, Brewer, 2019).

Over and above the Perry and Wise (1990) definition of public service motivation, many other definitions relate the concept to the public sector, to public organisations and to public employees (Piatak and Holt, 2020a). Indeed, around half of the 20 or so definitions cited by Barry Bozeman and Xuhong Su (2015) mention public employees, the public service, or the public sector.

Crucially, as explored in Chapter Five, almost all of the empirical research on public service motivation focuses on the public sector. Indeed, of the c150 articles published in 2020 around public service motivation, all but three were published in journals focusing on public administration or public management (and two of these three focused on public employees). For example, the highest number of articles published in a single journal in 2020 was 18, published in the *International Public Management Journal*. These included empirical research on public service motivation in fire fighters, police officers, public healthcare workers, public teachers, government agencies and local government employees. Two did not cover public employees, exploring public service motivation in Russian students (Gans-Morse et al, 2020), and in citizens in Catalonia, Spain (Ripoll and Schott, 2020). Any review of the empirical research on public service motivation would give the overwhelming impression that public service motivation is about public employees in the public sector, or at least is researched in terms of public employees.

Despite this clear theoretical and empirical focus on public employees and the public sector, many authors argue that public service motivation is not unique to the public sector.

Several suggest that public service motivation can be found in many individuals and across many sectors and settings (Vandenabeele, 2007; Liu et al, 2008; Pandey et al, 2008; Perry and Hondeghem, 2008), and there is a limited but growing empirical work examining public service motivation in the third or charitable sector (not-for-profit). There is also a small but growing interest in the public service motivated non-work activities of public employees.

The issue here is that this conflates, or at least confuses, state with society. It implicitly suggests that the two are interchangeable, and essentially the same. That anything that is not private is public, it is in the common domain, which equates to government, and that it is possible to distinguish between these two opposites. Much of the PSMT literature supposes that there are private interests and public interests; self-regarding motives and other regarding motives. This conflation is reflected both in several definitions of public service motivation, and in the measurement instruments used to empirically explore public service motivation.

Take, for example, Sangmook Kim's 14-item scale for measuring public service motivation (Kim, 2009), which builds on and further develops James Perry's original 24-item scale (Perry, 1996). Both scales include a number of statements about government work, and a number about community or society more generally. Kim's 14-item scale covers the four PSMT domains of attraction to public policy making, commitment to the public interest, compassion and self-sacrifice. The first two domains are clearly located in government and public service; as Adrian Ritz (2011) and many others have argued, public policy is a unique feature of government work, and individuals with a significant attraction to this kind of work are most likely to seek public employment. The public interest is an abstract and contested concept, but generally denotes society as a whole and is directly related to government and state.

These two domains in Kim's measurement scale contain six statements, which are set out in Table 2.1. Four of these

Table 2.1: Attraction to public policy making and commitment to public interest

Ref	Statement (taken from Kim, 2009)	Comment
Attraction to public policy making		
PSM1	'I am interested in making public programs that are beneficial for my country or the community I belong to.'	About public employment as means by which to contribute to clear, definable beneficiaries and to society as whole.
PSM2	'Sharing my views on public policies with others is attractive to me.'	Not related to public employment.
PSM3	'Seeing people get benefits from the public program I have been deeply involved in brings me a great deal of satisfaction.'	About public employment. Clear, definable beneficiaries.
Commitment to public interest		
PSM4	'I consider public service my civic duty.'	About public employment.
PSM5	'Meaningful public service is very important to me.'	About public employment.
PSM6	'I would prefer seeing public officials do what is best for the whole community even if it harmed my interests.'	Not related to public employment.

six statements are focused on public employment (public service). Two of these include references to clear, definable beneficiaries – PSM1 talks about policy benefits to the responder's own community, and PSM3 talks about the benefits to policy recipients. (The statement suggests that specific individuals benefit from a specific policy, and not that society as a whole benefits from public policies generally.) Two of the three statements in the commitment to public interest domain (PSM4 and PSM5) are about the value of public employment to the individual responder, and contain no reference to the goal or purpose of this employment. One statement (PSM6) could be a motivation for public employment, but equally would not necessitate any public sector behaviour.

Kim and colleagues further developed these domains in later work, publishing an international scale in 2013 that repositioned the two public domains as attraction to public service and commitment to public values (Kim et al, 2013). Of the eight statements in these two revised domains, only one is specifically about public employment (PSM3 in the attraction to public service domain, 'meaningful public service is very important to me'). This is confusing; Kim and colleagues do not define public service motivation in the article, beyond a single sentence that relates it directly to government work (p 80).

The compassion and self-sacrifice domains in Kim's 2009 scale include eight statements, all of which are unrelated to public employment, and are about our general concern for others. The statements included in the compassion domain generally relate to clear and specific beneficiaries, whereas the self-sacrifice domain includes four statements that each reference society as a whole. Taken together, the statements in Kim's 2009 14-item measurement scale mix state and society in a way that suggests these are confused or conflated. The later 2013 scale is clearly less focused on public employment, although has largely been used in empirical work to measure public service motivation in public employees.

Perry's 24–item scale (1996) is equally confused. This scale includes four domains, familiar to almost all of the PSMT literature. As with Kim's 2009 scale, Perry's scale includes four domains, two of which are government-focused. The attraction to public policy making includes three statements. Two of these relate to politics, and all are negatively construed. As discussed in Chapter Five, the framing of these statements, and of this particular aspect of public service motivation, has been contested and much criticised, and the domain has been revised and redeveloped since Perry first tested it. But consistent with most of the ways in which public service motivation is measured, the attraction to public policy making and commitment to public interest domains in Perry's measurement scale mix state and society, and conflate public employment and civic engagement.

Why is this important? Because if public service motivation is about public service through public employment – that is, is about *the call of public service* (Perry and Hondeghem, 2008), then its measurement needs to be about public employment. If, however, it is about any other regarding motives *regardless of setting*, then surely it needs to be measured in a way that does not make it dependent on public employment.

As they stand, several of the current measurement instruments are confusing. It is odd that an instrument that is focused on public sector employment, or framed in such a way that they make little sense to someone outside of the public sector, is used to ascertain levels of public service motivation in private or charitable sector employees. Such an approach would be bound to discover that public employees are indeed more public service motivated.

This point is made more eloquently by Gene A Brewer in his chapter on public service motivation in Andrew Massey's *A research agenda for public administration* (Brewer, 2019). Brewer is decisively in the camp asserting public service motivation as being about other regarding motives regardless of setting. He suggests that measurement scales increasingly focus on public sector employment in order to improve their validity and sensitivity, and points out that this makes research in other sectors more challenging.

This is particularly important because there is ongoing debate within the field about whether public service motivation is an aggregate of these domains, or whether each domain can be separately measured. In most of the empirical literature, it is measured as an aggregate; so that public employees are of course going to be observed to have higher levels of public service motivation because the measurement scales are weighted in their favour. But it is also significant because if the construct goes beyond public institutions and organisations – if public service motivation is simply about other regarding motives – then it needs to be conceptually distinct from a plethora of other related concepts, such as altruism and prosocial motives.

Altruism, prosocial behaviour and public service motivation

Public service motivation can be conceived as one in a family of other regarding motivations and behaviours. Altruism, community citizenship behaviour, organisational citizenship behaviour, prosocial motivation and prosocial behaviour are all part of this wider family. If public service motivation is not uniquely found in public servants and public institutions and organisations, but rather is a general human trait regardless of setting, then it is important that it be distinct to its fellow other regarding motives (Bozeman and Su, 2015). Related to this point, I would also argue that it is important to understand how different other regarding motives, as well as self-regarding motives, might affect public service motivated behaviours.

Two of the more significant other regarding motives I want to discuss here are altruism and prosocial motivation. There have been some recent attempts to examine the relationships between these motives and public service motivation, but others have added to the confusion. This is in part because these two concepts – and particularly altruism – are themselves challenging to define.

Altruism is a concept for which there is no commonly agreed definition. It is generally seen as both a motivation and a behaviour (Elster, 2006). Altruism is often contrasted with self-interested motivation and behaviour, or perhaps as part of a continuum of motivations. Actors are rarely either complete altruists or complete egotists (Piatak and Holt, 2020a), and indeed altruism can be self-regarding. Richard Jankowski (2015) argues that 'altruists derive utility when other people's wellbeing is increased as a result of their charity' (p 17), and therefore can be seen as being consistent with self-interest. He also argues that it must be group-specific (that is, there must be a clear set of beneficiaries). Elster (2006) states that there is a body of empirical evidence that demonstrates that altruistic behaviour might be generated by self-interested motivations. Indeed, at the extreme, it has been linked to narcissism (White et al, 2018; Fennimore, 2021), and more generally as a 'warm glow' or impure altruism (Andreoni, 1990). As with Jankowski's definition, warm glow altruism assumes that the actor gains some pleasure or utility from the altruistic act. Indeed, it has previously been argued that it is this warm glow altruism that underpins PSMT (O'Leary, 2019).

Altruism has been core to several definitions of public service motivation. Many equate public service motivation and altruism, and others assert there is a strong link (Piatak and Holt, 2020b). Such is the confusion that there have been at least three papers published in the last two years that have tried to clarify the difference between altruism and public service motivation. However, these papers add to the confusion, rather than clarify the situation.

Carina Schott and colleagues' (2019) recent paper aimed to provide conceptual clarity between public service motivation, prosocial motivation and altruism. They state that altruism is a behaviour rather than a motivation, which they argue is necessary because otherwise prosocial motivation and altruistic motivation would essentially be defined in the same way. Conceiving altruism in only behavioural terms is at odds with most of the wider literature, which sees it as both a type of motivation and behaviour. They then suggest that both prosocial motivation and public service motivation can generate altruistic behaviour; the difference being that prosocial motivation is about helping specific people or groups, whereas altruism generated by public service motivation is targeted at society as a whole.

Jaclyn Piatak and Stephen Holt have authored two recent papers aimed at disentangling altruism and public service motivation (2020a; 2020b). In contrast to Schott and colleagues, they argue that altruism is both a motivation and a behaviour, and that it is aimed at specific groups of people or beneficiaries and not at society as a whole. Whereas Schott and colleagues distinguish between public service motivation and altruism as motivation versus behaviour, Piatak and Holt do so in terms of the multidimensionality of public service motivation and the unidimensionality of altruism.

Nor is the relationship between altruism and public service motivation clearer from the empirical work. Both Kim's 2009 14-item scale, and Perry's 1996 24-item scale include a self-sacrifice domain. This domain is how altruism is operationalised in PSMT (Perry, 1996; Perry and Vandenabeele, 2015). The item statements in both scales are about society as a whole, rather than specific populations or groups, suggesting support for Schott and colleagues' notion of altruism in PSMT being about society at large. However, it also suggests that altruism is an antecedent motive of public service motivation, whereas Schott and colleagues see altruism as a behavioural outcome of public service motivation, and Piatak and Holt see it as a complementary other regarding motive and behaviour.

The situation is equally confusing with regards to prosocial motivation and behaviour. Several recent papers have attempted to provide clarity, differentiating between public service and prosocial motivators, but have again provided more confusion than clarity. Corduneanu and colleagues (2020) see both public service motivation and prosocial motivation as being future-, goal- and other-orientated; the key difference between the two is that public service motivation is about society at large, whereas prosocial motivation is about specific, identifiable beneficiaries. Yet in other research, public service motivation is evidenced as the antecedent to a number of prosocial behaviours with specific, identifiable beneficiaries, including disabled clients of physiotherapists (Andersen and Serritzlew, 2012), citizen service volunteering (Ward, 2019), specific types of organisational citizenship behaviour (Kim, 2006; Cheng et al, 2020), work that involves lots of direct interaction with clients (Christensen and Wright, 2011), and whistle-blowing (Davis et al, 2020), to name but a few.

Politicians

Public policy is not the only unique feature of government. Politicians and, in many countries in which PSMT work is undertaken, *elected* politicians, are also unique to government. That is not to say that all public organisations involve political leaders. Many public agencies do not directly involve politicians, and the links between political control and public agencies vary considerably. But politicians are only found in government, and make significant decisions that affect and are affected by the public sector. The public sector is also inherently political, making and implementing decisions about 'who gets what, when, how' (Lasswell, 1936). And yet politicians do not feature in definitions of PSMT, and (with a few exceptions, almost exclusively in relation to local government) are not a group of public servants covered by empirical work in the field. This gap is striking (Ritz, 2011; van der Wal, 2013; Ritz et al, 2016).

When politics is discussed, it is generally about the political activities of public employees (see, for example, Cooper, 2020, Kerrissey et al, 2020; van Acker, 2020 for recent examples). Or, politicians are seen as external actors, whose political and policy decisions are detrimental to the public service motivation of public employees (see, for example, Jensen et al, 2020). There is no mention of democracy, elections, or politicians in Perry and Hondeghem's edited book on public service motivation, nor any mention in James Perry's recently published monograph.

One of the few articles that examines politicians is a recently published empirical exploration of the effect of public service motivation on political candidacy. This article, published in an economics journal and authored by Alessandro Fedele and Pierpaolo Giannoccolo (2020), found that levels of public service motivation were important. Although this paper was first published in June 2019, it has yet to be cited in any of the PSMT literature.

A more substantive consideration given to politicians and public service motivation is by Lene Pedersen. Pedersen has published research on citizens' attitudes towards politicians' pay (Pedersen et al, 2019; Pedersen and Pedersen, 2020), political leadership (Pedersen et al, 2018a), and politicians' attitudes towards pay (Pedersen et al, 2018b). And she has also written on public service motivation in local councillors in Denmark (Pedersen, 2014). Pedersen starts her discussion with the assertion that is common to PSMT that Public Choice scholars see public actors as being rational *and* self-interested (2014: 886), citing Anthony Downs' *Economic theory of democracy* (1997 [1957]) as evidence of this. Pedersen examines the effects that two different prosocial motivations have on behaviours, namely commitment to the public interest and user orientation. She finds that councillors with higher levels of commitment to the public interest work longer hours, are more engaged in policy agenda setting, and see themselves as being more influential.

Zeger van der Wal (2013) uses qualitative interviews to compare the motivations of politicians and senior civil servants in the Netherlands and the United States (he does not say why he chose these two countries). He found both public servants and politicians expressed other regarding and self-regarding motives, although the latter reflected their different public service roles, concluding that politicians 'are motivated by being in power; whereas being close to power motivates administrative elites' (p 757). Boruvka and Perry (2020) do mention politicians, and perhaps give the game away as to how they are viewed in PSMT. In an article that compares the motivational assumptions of NPM and PSMT, they discuss the continuing use of NPM-type reforms in terms of political legitimacy. They suggest that this happens to 'maintain or reinforce who is in charge (that is, political masters rather than bureaucrats)' (p 578), and then go on to state:

> The continued strength of outsourcing is a good example of the survival of a key aspect of NPM even when it has failed to lower costs or improve effectiveness. In many jurisdictions, contracting is a substitute for past practices, such as patronage. Contracts are used to award political constituencies, much like jobs (i.e., membership/spoils) were once used to reward supporters who voted and worked on behalf of a politician. (p 578)

Take out the reference to NPM, and this could be a quote from almost any Public Choice work. It implies that politicians act instrumentally to further their self-interests, here being their likelihood of being re-elected. There is no suggestion of mixed motives, or that politicians might be seeking to further the public interest.

But these papers are by far the exception. As far as PSMT is concerned, politicians do not figure as public servants.

This is an odd omission. There is a significant body of research that demonstrates that good political leaders are fundamental to good government. Politics plays a key role in public policy making, in decisions about public values, public sector structure and organisations, public employee numbers, pay and benefits. If public service motivation is uniquely about public servants, then politicians should be a focus of theoretical or empirical research.

Public service or profession service motivation?

Not all public employees are expected to be motivated by other regarding intentions. At least, this is my impression from the gaps in the empirical research around public service motivation. Refuse collectors, hospital cleaners, security and building maintenance staff are public employees that have not yet been the subject of public service motivation research, and much of the language used in conceptualising public service motivation would seem to exclude these types of occupations from its scope. Indeed, the Attraction to Public Policy Making domain in many of the tools used to measure levels of public service motivation does not just discriminate against private-sector workers, but also against public-sector blue-collar workers, most of whom will be some distance from policy making.

This focus on professions creates two critical issues for PSMT; one of which is beginning to be recognised, the other is not.

Of course, it should be recognised here that the distinction between what is and what is not a profession is not a straightforward one. There have been several attempts to define the concept of professions, a task made difficult by unique differences between professions (Freidson, 1970), whether to focus on the attributes of professions (Greenwood, 1957), or more widely on their economic and political power (Freidson, 1986). So difficult is the task of defining the professions, that there is still significant debate about it (Modarresi et al, 2001), with at least one author suggesting that such attempts are essentially futile (Saks, 2012).

Professions themselves have set out what it means to be a profession, and it is these definitions which raise a critical issue for PSMT. Many professional bodies include *serving the public interest* in their defining characteristics. Two definitions from the medical profession include references to serving others. Cruess and colleagues (2004) state that a profession is a knowledge-based vocation that involves service to others. More recently, Tilburt (2014) argues that the public interest goes further than benefiting individual patients, but includes the wider public interest of just use of healthcare resources. References to serving the public, public service and the public interest resonate in many professions. Indeed, core to the argument here is that serving the wider public interest, of selflessness, is an important professional norm that is reflected in the motivations and behaviours of professions. Not only does this professions' focus on the public interest mirror that found in PSMT, but they also share this distinction between user orientation and wider, more abstract 'public'.

And herein lies the first crucial issue for PSMT. If the public interest is a core norm in professions, and professions are the key groups covered by PSMT empirical work, how can we be sure that public service motivation is not really professions service motivation? That observed levels of public service motivation and its effects on behavioural outcomes are not, in reality, evidence of professional norms?

Membership of a profession as a antecedent of public service motivation was first identified by James Perry in the late 1990s (Perry, 1997). More recently, Carina Schott and colleagues begin to touch upon this in a paper on decision making in dilemma situations (Schott et al, 2018). However, their focus is on professional identity, and their empirical lens is user orientation (in this case, decisions by individual vets in specific hypothetical dilemma situations). Indeed, they specifically exclude the wider public interest from their consideration of professional role identity.

That serving the public interest is an important professional norm is recognised in an earlier paper by Lotte Andersen and Soren Serritzlew (2012). The authors used a knowledge-based definition of professions, stating that a profession 'is an occupation with a high level of professionalism, defined as the degree of co-existence of specialized, theoretical knowledge and professional norm' (p 20). They go on to recognise the role of professional socialisation and the internalisation of professional norms of serving the public, and putting other regarding motives before personal gain. Their empirical work does examine commitment to the public interest, though their focus is on individual user orientation (in this case, decisions by Danish physiotherapists on care and treatment for individual disabled clients).

Importantly, the authors suggest that their 'theoretical argument concerning professions surely indicates that it could very well be different for non-professionals (because no professional norm would then regulate the use of services)' (Andersen and Serritzlew, 2012: 27). They also recognise that levels of professionalisation might affect the extent to which professional norms affect behaviour. Through qualitative interviews, they identify that professional norms exist within the Danish physiotherapy profession, and state that these norms are 'not as firm as for health occupations with very high levels of professionalism (e.g., dentists and physicians)' (p 22). Finally, the authors find no difference in the effect of commitment to the public interest on decisions about individual patients between private sector and public sector physiotherapists. The authors conclude that this finding demonstrates that public service motivation is not unique to the public sector. But they ignore that this might indicate that professional norms, rather than public service motivation, is the important driving force.

These papers aside, there is little recognition in the PSMT literature that professions' norms of serving the public might be a better explanation of what is being observed in empirical work. This provides further evidence to support the line of argument by Bozeman and Su (2015) that it is difficult to distinguish public service motivation from other service motivation studies.

More importantly, the second crucial issue for PSMT is not one that is explicitly recognised in the literature. This issue flows from Andersen and Serritzlew's observation that the extent of professionalisation will affect the behavioural power of professional norms. Professions are not static entities. Over the past 50 years or so, there has been a significant increase in most developed countries in the number of professions, and in the number of people practising those professions (Kleiner and Krueger, 2008; O'Leary, 2015), reflecting changes in the structure of labour markets and the structure of developed economies. And this increase has also led to an increase in the numbers and scope of state registration, licensing and regulation of professions.

Professions regulation is often described as being a social contract between the state and the professions, a 'regulatory bargain' (Cooper et al, 1988); so that the state guarantees a monopolistic right of practice, and in return, the profession agrees to service the public interest by only allowing competent and ethical individuals to practise the profession (MacDonald, 1995). While this is not a particularly convincing argument – professional norms of serving the public exist in many professions long before they are regulated by the state – the existence of this norm raises a significant challenge for PSMT. Because professionalisation can be seen as a process, including achieving state regulation, signals that the occupation has achieved a certain status, a level of specialism, expertise and knowledge and, for individuals within the group, a means by which they signal their membership of a professional organisation and qualifications (O'Leary, 2015). It incentivises action by individuals, professional bodies, and others. It is an important part of professional identity, and it is an important work and service motivator.

This raises significant questions for PSMT. It suggests mixed motives underplaying the professionalisation process, which will not be captured by PSMT research because: (a) almost all PSMT research utilises cross-sectional designs, and thus does not pick up change over time; (b) that the norm of commitment to serving the public might have self- and other regarding foundations; and (c) that PSMT needs to consider alternative explanations for its empirical observations.

Finally, because of its overwhelming focus on professions, there is something quite elitist about PSMT, both in how it is framed and how it is researched. The *call to public service* is considered to be a higher, more noble, more worthy pursuit than working in the private sector or working for extrinsic rewards such as pay and pensions.

Intrinsic motivation

Might public employees be motivated by the enjoyment they get from their work and, if so, is this consistent with public service motivation?

As the concept and empirical measurement of public service motivation have developed and changed over the past 30 years, so has the role that intrinsic motivation plays in PSMT changed and developed. A quick comparison of the indices of two major books on public service motivation, published 13 years apart, gives some insight here. In *Motivation in public management* (Perry and Hondeghem, 2008), there are 30 references to intrinsic motivation and intrinsic reward. In *Managing organizations* (Perry, 2021), there is just one. While these two books may have different objectives, the scale of the difference highlighted here is interesting.

Intrinsic motivators are derived from undertaking the action itself, because of the enjoyment or interest generated from the action, the 'inherent tendency to seek out novelty and challenges, to extend and exercise one's capacities, to explore, and to learn' (Ryan and Deci, 2000: 70). They are often contrasted with extrinsic motivators, where the goal or results are separate from activity. Extrinsic motivators might be self-determined (Deci and Ryan, 1985). Working to benefit society might be an example of self-determined extrinsic motivator. They might also be externally determined, and it is these kinds of extrinsic motivations – particularly performance-related pay – that 'stand in opposition to the view that public service motives energize and direct the behavior [*sic*] of civil servants' (Perry and Wise, 1990: 367). Indeed, extrinsic rewards (particularly financial rewards) might 'crowd out' and lead to a decline in intrinsic motivation because they reduce the meaningfulness of the work being undertaken (Perry, 2021). This 'crowding out' argument is not unique to PSMT, with several economists making similar arguments (see, for example, the work of Bruno S. Frey in his 1997 book, *Not just for the money: an economic theory of personal motivation*).

Much PSMT work on public service motivation suggests it involves, or is related to, intrinsic motivators. Crewson (1997), Houston (2000), Kim (2006), Park and Rainey (2008), Koehler and Rainey (2008), Wright and Grant (2010), Caillier (2014), Jensen et al (2019) and Corduneanu et al (2020), have all defined public service motivation in terms of intrinsic motivators. Intrinsic motivation is also inherent in two commonly used measurement scales. In their original article on public service motivation, Perry and Wise (1990) made clear that the attraction to policy making would involve intrinsic motivation, as participation in the process of making policy would be 'exciting, dramatic, and reinforcing of an individual's image of self-importance' (p 369). And both the Perry (1996) and Kim (2009) survey instruments include an item in the self-sacrifice domain that clearly references intrinsic motivation; 'serving other citizens *would give me a good feeling even if no one paid me for it*' (emphasis added). This suggests that the public service motivation includes intrinsic drivers.

Indeed, intrinsic motivation is core to Deci and Ryan's (1985) self-determination theory, which played a key role in the development of PSMT (Perry, 2021). And, as Jaclyn Piatak and Stephen Holt have recently stated(2020b), public service motivation is 'a multimotive concept encompassing both self-regarding and other regarding motives' (p 504). Thus, a self-regarding motive such as intrinsic motivation could be consistent with the concept of public service motivation.

But others have thrown cold water on the idea and downplayed the role of intrinsic motivation with PSMT (Bozeman and Su, 2015). Wouter Vandenabeele in particular has argued that public service motivation is distinct from and does not include intrinsic motivators (Vandenabeele et al, 2018; Schott et al, 2019; Vandenabeele and Jager, 2020), because 'public service motivation leans heavily on the idea of public values being realized rather than enjoyment being gained' (Vandenabeele and Jager, 2020: 3). As such, several authors claim that public service motivation is distinct from other prosocial motivations, and from intrinsic motivation, although this appears to be a minority view within the field.

The argument put forward by this minority that public service motivation does not involve intrinsic drivers is not a convincing one. Public service motivation is just one of a family of other regarding motives and behaviours. This family includes altruism, organisational citizenship behaviour, community citizenship behaviour, prosocial motivation and prosocial behaviour. As already touched upon, the relationships and distinctiveness of these is subject to much debate. However, the issue here is that other forms of other regarding motives and behaviours can be driven and influenced by, and related to, intrinsic concerns. In particular, other regarding behaviours can involve intrinsic motivators. For example, organisational citizenship behaviour (OCB) (Organ, 1988) is a workplace-based prosocial behaviour that involves employees undertaking extra-role activities to benefit others in the workplace. It has multiple and overlapping motives, including intrinsic motivators (Finkelstein, 2011). There are strong links between this form of prosocial behaviour and public service motivation (Ingrams, 2020).

There is a growing body of research which finds that prosocial behaviour can be intrinsically motivated, with recent empirical work by Liu and colleagues (2019) and Wu and Jin (2020) for example, and several authors also link prosocial motivation and intrinsic motivation. Prosocial motivation is the 'desire to protect and promote the wellbeing of others' (Grant and Berg, 2010). Several authors suggest that prosocial motivation is a particular form of intrinsic motivation (Grant, 2008) and might be self-regarding (Bolino and Grant, 2016). Research suggests that intrinsic motivation is important to sustain prosocial motivation (Grant and Berg, 2010). This is perhaps related to empirical evidence that suggests that prosocial behaviour reduces with repetition (Meier, 2006), suggesting that prosocial motivation alone is not sufficient to sustain prosocial behaviour.

This raises two issues for PSMT. First, excluding intrinsic motivators from public service motivation would make it an outlier in terms of the family of other regarding motivations. If public service motivation is indeed one of the family of other regarding motivations, it should either be consistently conceptualised, or there needs to be a robust theoretical justification for if being differently conceptualised. The mainstream PSMT argument – that intrinsic motivation is consistent with public service motivation – is more defendable. Second, much PSMT empirical research on the consequences of public service motivation suggests that it is a driving force of public service motivated behaviours. But it is not the only motivator. It is repeatedly recognised in the PSMT literature that public employees might be motivated by a number of factors, of which public service motivation is just one. I would argue therefore (as many in the PSMT field do) that intrinsic motivation plays a fundamental role in the motivation of public sector employees.

Conclusion

It has been six years since Barry Bozeman and Xuhong Su (2015) concluded that the 'precondition for PSM's improved explanatory power is continued progress in conceptual development' (p 707). Although some progress has been made, there is a lot left to do. Some of the areas of conceptual confusion identified by Bozeman and Zu remain confused; indeed, with regards to the relationship between public service motivation and altruism, I would argue that matters are even more confused today than in 2015. It is also still not clear whether public service motivation is a specific type of prosocial motivation observable in public organisations and institutions, or a more general prosocial motivation. While it is obviously normatively attractive to widen the scope of public service motivation so that it is found in more and more contexts, taking it outside of public organisations raises some significant questions about the role that institutional settings play.

Perhaps this is to be expected? Many social science concepts are poorly conceptualised, contested and need further development. Is it realistic to expect something different from public service motivation? Maybe not. But given the scale of empirical work being published around public service motivation, it is essential that further conceptual and theoretical clarity is provided. Otherwise, how can it be claimed that what is being observed is indeed public service motivation?

THREE

The public in public service motivation theory

Introduction

One of the oldest and dominant views of government work is that there is no finer, or more noble, calling than public service. Through public service, individuals put aside their own interests and work to further the greater good. Barry Bozeman (2007) explains that the public interest is a means of 'conceptualising, explaining, and, sometimes, prescribing collective good' (p 86), and discussions of the common good, of public values, and of the public interest have been core to political debate for many centuries.

It is also the case that the *public interest* plays a pivotal role in PSMT. Indeed, for many, the basis of public service motivation is a personal desire to further the public interest. Given this, PSMT should be expected to be able to address some basic questions:

- How do public servants define and understand the public interest?
- How do they identify what is in the public interest?

- How do they test this with the public?
- How do they respond when their actions are not supported by the public?

This chapter considers these questions. It starts by discussing the concept of the public interest, what it means and how it is understood. It then considers the role that the public interest plays in PSMT. The argument developed here is that it plays a pivotal role, and as such questions about how PSMT specifies how public service-motivated public servants understand, seek to further, make decisions around how to, and know whether they have, furthered the public interest are core to an evaluation of the usefulness and completeness of PSMT.

Defining the public interest

The public interest is the dominant language of public employees, politicians and governments (O'Leary, 2019). It has a long and veritable tradition, and appears in the works of political philosophers from Plato onwards (Held, 1970). While its importance as an academic concept has changed over the last 80 years, the idea of the *public interest* nevertheless has enduring appeal. It has been core to many debates, within and without academia; politicians, public servants, professions and the courts all draw on the public interest to promote and justify their actions and decisions. It is the 'first and oldest theory' of government regulation (Yandle, 2011), a core and significant area of government activity and an area where public interest theory is most developed. Although the concept of the public interest fell out of favour in some circles during the middle of the 20th century, it is nevertheless the case that 'public interest theory never goes away' (Bozeman, 2007).

There is a significant literature on the public interest, with many books, articles and blogs devoted to the concept. It is particularly well covered in the area of government regulation, for example. The literature is too substantive to be covered in depth here, but the key question that needs addressing is how the public interest is understood in PSMT. Specifically, if public service motivation is the desire to further the public interest, how does PSMT theorise how public service-motivated individuals understand the public interest, and how they understand whether they are furthering the public interest? If the public interest is so core to an individual's public service motivation, then surely PSMT should be able to answer these questions.

Before turning to PSMT, it is worth briefly outlining more generally how the public interest is conceptualised. To do so, I will draw on three general works in the field, namely: (a) Clarke Cochran's seminal 1974 article, 'Political science and "the public interest"'; (b) Barry Bozeman's 2007 book *Public values and public interest: counterbalancing economic individualism*; and, (c) because it is a field in which public interest theory is most developed, Steven P Croley's *Regulation and public interests* (2008). Understanding how the public interest is generally understood, and examining it within a specific area of government activity – regulation – should enable an understanding of some of the issues and challenges faced by PSMT in conceptualising how public service-motivated public employees might work in the public interest.

Despite (or perhaps because of) its endless appeal, the public interest is poorly defined and conceptualised, with many competing attempts to set out what it means. It is a term that is full of expectation and appeal to a better world, but it is also used to justify specific actions, decisions and government interventions. There is a long and complex history of attempts to define and understand the concept (Simm, 2011). Several reviews of the literature have identified differences in how the concept is defined. It is often treated simply as a fact of democratic government (Jordan, 2007). Because of this complexity and the competing understandings, several writers have suggested that attempts to define and operationalise the concept should be abandoned, and others have simply not attempted to define it. Others have questioned whether there is such a thing as a public interest theory (Hantke-Domas, 2003), that it is largely meaningless, or suggested that it can simply be rejected as being based on naïve assumptions (Christensen, 2011).

However, there are three specific meanings or uses of the concept of the public interest that can be identified in the literature. These are the public interest: (a) as an ideal; (b) as an administrative process; and (c) as a justification for action.

The public interest as an ideal

This is perhaps the more pervasive conception of the public interest. Here, the public interest is a normative concept, an ideal, a goal of serving the interests of the whole community or general public. In this conception, the public interest does not have any specific content; rather it is a general aim that public officials and employees should pursue. It is also a means by which policies and programmes can be evaluated. It is about 'outcomes best serving the long term survival and wellbeing of a social collective known as "the public"' (Bozeman, 2007) or, more generally, on furthering social welfare. This view of the public interest sees serving it as being a higher, more nobler calling than the baser, nastier, serving of self or group interests, to which it is often contrasted.

The public interest here is not simply about aggregating individual interests. Rather, it is an assumption that the whole is greater than the parts. There is debate about whether the interests of all of the public need to be furthered, or whether some individuals losing out is acceptable if the overall good is furthered. There is reference in some of the literature to utilitarianism in considering how the overall public interests might be understood, and there is sometimes the assertion that the public interest is simply a reflection of the programmes of democratically elected governments. But while this view of the public interest rejects the notion, which they associated with Public Choice, of individual and group interests competing with each other to influence government decisions, it has little to say on how these different publics are actually identified and served.

Indeed, this conception of the public interests lacks much content, so that it is impossible to understand exactly what this means in practice. This is perhaps inevitable given that it is a normative ideal. But it is important because it is the normative aspect of the public interest that is core to PSMT; for serving the public interest is the core normative aspect of public service motivation (Perry and Wise, 1990).

The public interest as an administrative process

Much recent work on the public interest has tended to steer away from attempts to define it as an abstract concept, and rather focus on the formal procedures used in decision-making. But such an approach is also found in older discussions about the public interest, and was identified by Clarke Cochran (1974) in his typology of public interest theories, and his defence of the concept of the public interest. In this article, Cochran identifies process theories as ones that accept the usefulness of the concept, but which typically reject the notion of the public interest as a normative ideal or the ultimate goal of public policy. These approaches deny the existence of a single, coherent, public interest – Cochran explains that they 'find many "publics" rather than one community or public and many interests rather than one interest held by the community' (p 339).

It is because these theories acknowledge the existence of many, sometimes competing, 'publics' that they focus on the process of decision-making. Specifically, they focus on the process by which consensus might be found between these different interests. Cochran starts by discussing utilitarianism as a 'process' approach, referencing the works of Jeremy Bentham, and which conceives of the public interest as the sum of the aggregation of individual interests. He dismisses this approach, arguing that it has few current adherents. He also considers, and largely rejects, other definitions of the public interest as the outcome of the political process.

More recent work on the public interest focuses on the process by which all stakeholders are involved in decision-making. Such approaches are exemplified by Steven P Croley in his book on *Regulation and public interests* (2008). These definitions are not interested in the results or outcome in government decision-making. Rather, on the broadness of the different interests involved, the procedures used and the openness of the decision-making.

The public interest as justification for action

The third category of definitions of the public interest are what I call justifications for action. This is perhaps the closest that public interest theories get to addressing Schubert's point of describing a relationship between a concept of the public interest and the actual behaviour of public servants (Schubert, 1957). Earlier conceptions of this drew on Woodrow Wilson's politics–administration dichotomy (Wilson, 1887), and again echoed the view that in democratic societies, the public interest is synonymous with the programmes of elected governments, acting on voters' mandates, and implemented by the bureaucracy.

More recent work that sees the public interest as justification for action can be found in theoretical and empirical examination of public values. Barry Bozeman (2007) states that public values are the 'normative principles on which governments and policies should be based and thus provide direction to the behaviour of public servants' (p 13). He goes on to state that: 'public values are those providing normative consensus about (1) the rights, benefits, and prerogatives to which citizens should (and should not) be entitled, (2) the obligations of citizens to society, the state, and one another, and (3) the principles on which governments and policies should be based' (p 132). Public values approaches are normative in nature. But unlike theories that see the public interest as an ideal, public values approaches provide content and specificity around what this really means. This is because public values are expected to provide direction to the behaviour and actions of public servants; providing a set of principles or expected outcomes that should be followed by public servants when developing a public service or publishing new regulations (Andersen et al, 2013). Public value approaches also build on theories that see the public interest as an administrative process, accepting that there might be value conflicts, and that values will differ between policies and programmes.

However, there are still significant issues with public values approaches. The concept is contested, and is still under-conceptualised (Meynhardt and Jasinenko, 2020). There are some striking similarities between public values and other approaches, including PSMT (Andersen et al, 2013). There is also a dearth of empirical evidence; the evidence that is available focuses on public managers and leaders, and is single-case study-based (Hartley et al, 2017).

There are two other issues with incorporating public values into an understanding of how public employees discern the public will. The first is the confusion between society and state discussed in the previous chapter. Swapping the abstract concept of the public interest with the more concrete content of public values does not resolve this fundamental issue. Because public values, as perceived by Barry Bozeman, mix the values, rights and responsibilities of society and state.

Bozeman recognised this when he posed questions about the meaning of publicness, and particularly whether 'public values attach to political action, to public authority, or to more deeply seated prerogatives of the governed?' (Jorgensen and Bozeman, 2007: 355). But second, public values here are seen as universal at the state/society level. There is no recognition of differences within the state in public values, and the conflict these might generate. So, for example, the public values of national security and individual rights – different parts of the state might see these values differently, might privilege one over the other, might not focus on at all of the first. (Jorgensen and Bozeman (2007) provide a hierarchical list of public values, drawn from a literature review. National security and defence of the realm are not listed as public values.) As with PSMT, the public values narrative makes an assumption that the public sector is a single, homogeneous entity with shared, common values.

Varieties of publics and public interests

The concept of the public interest is often invoked by politicians, judges, lawyers, professional bodies, lobbyists and public servants. And occasionally, by ordinary voters too. So it is perhaps to be expected that a concept such as the public interest would engender such debate. That there is not a single, coherent and commonly agreed definition of the public interest is not, in of itself, an issue. Nor is it necessarily problematic that there are different typologies available of the various public interest theories. Indeed, I would suggest that each of us has our own understanding of what constitutes the public interest, and our own assessments of whether governments, public policies and public services are satisfying those understandings. But given its centrality to PSMT (as evidenced next), it is important to understand which of these approaches to understanding the public interest, why, and to what effect, PSMT draws upon.

The public interest and public service motivation theory

At the beginning of this chapter, I stated that the public and the public interest play a pivotal role in PSMT. This assertion is evidenced here, as it is the basis of one of my fundamental criticisms of PSMT.

Several definitions relate public service motivation, either directly or indirectly, to serving or furthering the public interest. Direct references are made by a large number of scholars in their definitions of public service motivation. Carina Schott and colleagues state that public service motivation is seen as a 'personal commitment to serving the public interest' (Schott et al, 2018), and Lois Wise argues that public service motivation is about individuals' promoting the public interest (Wise, 2000). Leonard Bright (2008) argues that public service motivations are the 'altruistic intentions that motivate individuals to service the public interest' (p 151), and definitions by Taylor (2008) and Scott and Pandey (2005) all make a direct connection between the public interest and public service motivation.

There are also several definitions that, while not directly identifying the public interest, do make reference to serving the common good, the public will, community or society as a whole. In the preface to their book, *Motivation in public management: the call of public service*, James Perry and Annie Hondeghem (2008) state the public service motivation is: 'an individual's orientation to delivering public services to people with a purpose to do good for others and society' (p vii). Rainey and Steinbauer (1999) refer to it as: 'a general, altruistic motivation to serve the interest of a community of people, a state, a nation or humankind' (p 20). Wolter Vandenabeele (2007) states that public service motivation is: 'the belief, values and attitudes that go beyond self-interest and organizational interest, that concern the interest of a larger political entity and that motivate individuals to act accordingly whenever appropriate' (p 549). In a critical review of the concept of public service motivation, Barry Bozeman and Xuhong Su (2015) identify 23 different definitions of public service motivation. Of these, three directly associated it with the public interest, and almost all make some reference to public service, helping the community, altruism or prosocial motives.

Further evidence of the importance of the concept of the public interest to PSMT can be found in James Perry's (1996) PSM measurement scale. This was the first survey method developed to measure public service motivation. Perry originally proposed 40 statements, organised in six domains or dimensions, to measure levels of public service motivation. Of these original six domains, two directly related to the public interest, namely *commitment to the public interest* and *civic duty* (Perry, 1996) although there was crossover between the two. (For example, the *public interest* domain included the statement 'I consider public service my civic duty'.)

This proposed scale was eventually published as a four-domain construct consisting of 24 statements. Two of these domains directly relate to acting selflessly in the interests of other people (Weißmüller et al, 2020) and one, the revised *commitment to the public interest* domain, is specifically about serving the public interest, which contains five statements.

These statements include references to community, public service and civic duty. Several make clear that the public interest means putting others before self. Indeed, in PSM8 – 'I would prefer seeing public officials do what is best for the whole community even if it harmed my interests' (Perry, 1996), Perry again suggests that public service motivation is the opposite of rational self-interest, a theme that arises in a number of the other statements in the other domains, particularly in the self-sacrifice domain. Almost all of the statements that make up the self-sacrifice domain include a comparison between public or other regarding, and self-interested motivations. And while there have been several other scales proposed, and many revisions made to Perry's scale (Kim, 2009), all include references to the serving or furthering of the public interest in some form or another.

Defining the public interest in public service motivation theory

Despite the pivotal role that the public interest plays in PSMT and in definitions of public service motivation, PSMT provides little explanation about how public servants go about 'discerning and pursuing the public will' (Perry and Hondeghem, 2008). I have previously argued (2019), PSMT does not provide a clear definition of what constitutes the public interest, and how public employees might understand the public interest. It fails to provide any insight into how public employees might reconcile their individual conceptions of the public interest with group/organisational/political conceptions, or indeed how public employees receive feedback from, and respond to, the public to ensure their work does indeed further the public will. As Lene Pedersen stated in her 2014 article on public service motivation in politicians: 'the limited focus on how PSM influences the processes contributing to the definition of the public interest is rather surprising' (Pedersen, 2014: 886).

There are three possible routes through which public employees might discern the public will. Each of these routes is either briefly mentioned in the PSMT literature, or would be consistent with the tenets of PSMT and concepts of the public interest set out previously in this chapter.

The focus here is on public employees. For while there is a growing trend in the PSMT literature to assert that public service motivation is a universal motivation that transcends sector boundaries, it is still very much the case that the most commonly used definition is one that is centred on public institutions and organisations. And, as explored in Chapter Five, PSMT is very much about public employees; the motivations of elected officials, of politicians, is largely missing from the theoretical and empirical PSMT literature. (Indeed, Brewer, Selden and Facer (2000) suggest that public service-motivated public employees have 'a distaste for politics and politicians' (p 260)).

The three potential approaches explored here are: (a) that public employees are public stewards, entrusted by the public to further the public will; (b) that public employees understand the public interest to be outlined by the programmes of democratically elected governments (the politics–administration dichotomy); and (c) that PSMT does not need a developed explanation of how public employees understand the public interest.

Public stewards

Perry and Hondeghem (2008) suggest that because 'public servants are general altruists, then we (the public) will be inclined to rely on them to do good at all times' (p 8). David Houston, in one of the few considerations of the public in PSMT, draws on stewardship theory and argues that the public see civil servants as 'virtuous, committed caretakers, entrusted with the administration of the commons, guided by the will of the people' (Houston et al, 2007). In this view, the public see civil servants as trusted, benevolent stewards of the public good. Stewardship theory, which Houston draws on, is an approach to understanding governance that was applied to government by Thomas Schillemans (2013). And this trust should go both ways, with public service-motivated employees trusting the public, so that 'commitment to the public interest as norm-based PSM, compassion, and self-sacrifice as affective PSM can improve civil servants' trust in citizens' (Chen et al, 2014).

While Christopher Cooper and Tyler Reinagel (2017) do not refer to stewardship theory, they do suggest that trust in public employees is higher than trust in government, and that this is indicative of 'a sense of commonality/camaraderie in appreciation of government processes, even though outcomes and end-objectives vary greatly' (p 1300). That the public (and politicians) should simply trust that public servants work for the public good is also discussed by Julian Le Grand (2003;

2010), who sets out four different approaches to managing public service delivery (trust, mistrust, voice and choice). Le Grand also does not refer to stewardship theory, and the trust model he outlines does not include any reference to the public as trustees. Rather, the model assumes that politicians should simply trust public service professionals, let them get on with their jobs, and the public interest will be served.

This is a very underdeveloped part of PSMT, and raises several questions. In particular, it does not provide any specificity about how public service-motivated employees know how to 'do good at all times', as Perry and Hondeghem (2008) assert, or how they know what 'the will of the people' is as Houston et al (2007) argues. For how does a public service-motivated employee know what is good, what is the public's will?

Indeed, as with the focus on public sector professionals, there is something quite elitist in the (albeit limited) discussion of the public in public service motivation. Public servants know best; they know what is in the public's best interest (even if the public do not), and should simply be trusted. The trust model could be renamed as the deference model; we the public should simply defer to public servants as always knowing what is in our best interests.

But as William Niskanen (1971) observed nearly 50 years ago, public employees are 'neither omniscient nor sovereign' (p 39), because they cannot 'acquire all the information ... necessary to divine the public interest'. They face the same knowledge problems as everyone else, and as such: 'It is impossible for any one bureaucrat to act in the public interest, because of the limits of his [sic] information and the conflicting interests of others' (p 39). Mark Prebble (2016) argues that this is not a controversial conclusion to draw, stating that: 'It follows that if the public good is unknowable, there is likely to be disagreement about what is in the public interest' (p 247). Indeed, PSMT acknowledges that there will be such disagreement about the public interest, that there are different publics with different interests. Perry and Wise (1990) recognise that there is no single, coherent 'public' but different groups with different interests, and may act to further the interests of certain groups (perhaps to the detriment of other groups). It is also the case that public service-motivated civil servants will have ideas about what constitutes good policy, what public policy should look like and how they want to shape that policy.

The argument that public employees are simply trusted by citizens to further the public interest, and that public servants are thus entrusted, and know how to do good is therefore not convincing. It is not a fully developed thesis, and ignores the realities of different publics with different interests, and of information problems associated with understanding these different public wills.

Politics-administration dichotomy

A second potential explanation might be found in Woodrow Wilson's (1887) politics-administration dichotomy (Chen et al, 2013; O'Leary, 2019). Wilson's thesis, echoing Max Weber's *Economy and society* (1978) is often interpreted in two ways that are relevant to the discussion here. First, there is a distinction between politics and policy, with an assumption that the implementation and administration of policy are not political matters. This distinction reflects a 'logical and indispensable need to separate political goal setting from its administrative implementation' (Roman, 2017: 104). The second is that implementation and administration are the realm of public administrations, whereas politics is the realm of politicians. Public administrators are unbiased, neutral, competent and professional, often assumed to have no political preferences of their own, but rather implement the policy decisions of politicians and elected governments.

Applying the politics-administration dichotomy approach to understanding how public servants understand, interpret and apply the public interest would see civil servants take direction from politicians about what constitutes the public interest. In this view, politicians in democratic states, acting on a mandate from the public (voters), interpret the public interest. In a representative democracy, the programmes of elected governments would be the practical and real interpretations of the public interest. As such, PSMT would not require an explicit model or set of hypotheses about how public servants go about discerning the will of the public; the public interest is simply what elected governments do. Public servants are 'accountable through and to political authorities and the law' (Horton, 2008: 23) and in the context of the UK and the Westminster model, it means that the civil service's core characteristics are 'partisan neutrality, anonymity, and accountability to and through ministers' (p 23).

There are, however, three core problems with this approach.

First, there is a significant literature, spanning over half a century, which questions the normative naivety of the politics-administration dichotomy. Civil servants are not just neutral, disinterested implementors of political policy decisions; they are activity engaged in policy formation and decision-making. They can have significant discretion about 'who gets what, when, how' (Lasswell, 1936), either through active engagement in the policy process, or through their roles as street level bureaucrats (Lipsky, 1980). Public administration is an inherently political process.

Second, the politics-administration dichotomy is not discussed directly in the PSMT literature (O'Leary, 2019). There are a few vague, implicit references that might be construed as support for this approach. Sandra Horton's assertion, previously cited, that public employees are 'accountable through and to political authorities and the law' (Horton, 2008: 23) and David Houston's claim that public employees are 'virtuous, committed caretakers, entrusted with the administration of the commons, guided by the will of the people' (Houston et al, 2007: 2), for example, might be construed as an assertion of the politics–administration dichotomy. Lotte Andersen has argued that furthering the public interest is 'a public value, but we obviously need more concrete values specifying what serving society should include' (Andersen et al, 2013), and goes on to argue that public administrators need a clear set of public values, conceivably established by elected governments, that specify what the public interest is and means. But this would be a stretch. While the dichotomy might explain the lack of consideration of how public service-motivated public employees might discern the will of the public, it is not an explanation that has been proposed, adopted, or even considered within PSMT. There is an explicit reference to the dichotomy in the conclusions of a paper by Coursey and colleagues (2008), with reference to the 'attraction to policy making' domain within Perry's (1996) measurement scale. Coursey and colleagues suggest that public employees accept and desire a separation between politics and administration. However, this domain was not included in the construct validity tests, and it is not clear on what basis Coursey and colleagues draw this conclusion.

Indeed, there is evidence to suggest that some within PSMT overtly and explicitly reject the politics–administration dichotomy, and assert the role of public employees as essentially a political one. Mark Prebble (2016) identifies a number of assertions in PSMT about the role of public servants that he argues that, while laudable, are inherently both political and Political. Prebble identifies a number of normative public interest ideals that he suggests are associated with those on the political left. And from its earliest development, PSMT has recognised that public employees' attraction to policy making might be because they want to promote the interests of specific groups, or because they 'obtain benefits from effecting what they consider positive changes in public policy' (Gailmard, 2010); that is, public servants have policy preferences of their own and seek to further them.

More significantly, there is a small but growing body of work that assumes that there will be instances in which public service-motivated public employees will reject, undermine and actively work against policies, programmes and organisational changes, even if these are implemented by democratically elected governments. That is, when public employees believe that the programmes of elected governments are not what they perceive to be the public interest, it is consistent with their public service motivation to act against those programmes.

Most of the PSMT literature around change asserts a positive relationship between levels of public service motivation and acceptance of, or support for, policy change and public sector reform. There are, however, a small number of authors who challenge this assumption. So, for example, in an examination of the role of public service motivation in support for public service reform, Wright and colleagues (2013) assert that employees with higher levels of public service motivation will support policy changes 'that improve government services and benefit the public' (p 739). But they go on to state that: 'Unfortunately, such positive perceptions of organizational change may be the exception rather than the rule given the prevalence of concerns that public management reforms may lower the quality of government services and put the public at greater risk' (p 740). They then argue whether public service-motivated employees support policy or organisational change: 'requires the tenuous assumption that the employees trust the organization in which they work or that the proposed change is doing what is in the best interest of the public' (p 741). In other words, public employees can reject the policies and programmes of elected governments if they believe these are not consistent with their own views of what is in the public interest.

In a recent article on how policy change affected levels of public service motivation in Danish doctors, Ulrich Jensen and colleagues (2020) state that: 'PSM can be associated with politically initiated changes in the sense that PSM can act as a mobilizing force for supporting *certain* policies' (p 469, emphasis added). While Jensen and colleagues are examining the effect that negatively perceived policy changes have on levels of public service motivation, the implication here is that some policy changes are less likely to be supported than others. This conditional support is irrespective of whether the changes are a result of elected governments' programmes; that is, PSMT does not assume that the public interest is simply what is done by elected governments.

In another recently published article, Kristina Weißmüller and colleagues (Weißmüller et al, 2020) examine the role of public service motivation in what they term prosocial rule breaking. They start from an observation that a core public value is the principle of non-discrimination between citizens by the public sector. They go on to argue that the 'desire to help could be misapplied in a way that challenges public values; ... high-PSM individuals reveal a higher tendency than their low-PSM counterparts to break the rules in favor [*sic*] of citizens they believe need and deserve help and support' (p 2). Weißmüller and colleagues then go on to contrast prosocial rule breaking with actions that are self-interested, providing examples of where public service-motivated public employees might 'break the rules for noble causes' (p 5). Through three empirical studies, they find some support for these hypotheses. Finally, Potipiroon and Wongpreedee (2020) suggest that levels of public service motivation may be important in terms of whistle-blowing.

No need to define the public interest

The third and final potential explanation for the lack of consideration of the public and the public interest in PSMT is that offered through comparisons of public service motivation and the related concepts. In a recent article by Carina Schott and colleagues, the authors seek to spell out the difference between public service motivation, altruism and prosocial motivation. The authors examine this through qualitative research, itself unusual for PSMT empirical work, which is generally quantitative in nature.

Schott and colleagues compare and contrast these three motivations in three areas: beneficiaries; temporal focus; and changes in human action. They identify altruism as a type of behaviour rather than motivation, and argue that altruism might be the result of both prosocial and public service motivations. They differentiate prosocial motivation and public service motivation by suggesting that the beneficiaries of prosocial motivation are more direct – individuals or groups, or an organisation, with which the motivated individual is in direct contact, that it is the interpersonal connection that motivates prosocial behaviour. They compare this with the beneficiaries of public service-motivated individuals, which are more distant as they are 'society at large'. Because of this, a key difference between prosocial motivation and public service motivation is feedback; prosocial-motivated individuals can receive feedback and appreciation from recipients, whereas Schott and colleagues (2019) argue that: 'Society at large as a service recipient, however, does not provide direct feedback and express feelings of appreciation on a regular basis' (p 1201). This point is echoed by Wouter Vandenabeele and Stefanie Jager (2020), who argue that 'other types of prosocial motivation aim at a direct or reciprocal relationship with the beneficiary providing direct and identifiable benefits, whereas public service motivation does not involve this feedback mechanism since the beneficiary is unidentified' (p 3). Schott and colleagues also distinguish between prosocial and public service motivations by the temporal focus, suggesting that public service motivation is focused on the very long term.

This would suggest that the public and the public interest are both very abstract concepts in PSMT. It seems at odds with other work by Andersen and colleagues (2013) and Sangmook Kim and colleagues (2013) that reframe the concept of public interest as commitment to public values. This suggests a greater degree of specificity and granularity, but no detail is provided in how public service-motivated employees understand and translate these values.

Conclusion

The *public* and the *public interest* play pivotal roles in PSMT. Indeed, for many, the basis of public service motivation is a personal desire to further the public interest. Given this, PSMT should be able to address some basic questions about how public servants understand the public interest, consider different publics and different interests, get feedback from the public and understand whether they have indeed furthered the public interest.

PSMT does not provide this insight, avoiding any attempt to operationalise how public service-motivated public servants discern the public will. There is a significant body of PSMT theoretical and empirical literature that sets out the kinds of behaviours that should be expected from public service-motivated public employees – that they are compelled to seek employment in public organisations, that whistle-blowing and prosocial rule breaking behaviours are more likely, that performance and retention are related and that they will engage in organisation citizenship behaviour. But this literature does not address the fundamental question of how they understand and seek to further the public interest.

This is a significant gap in the literature, which poses fundamental challenges for PSMT.

First, the focus of most PSMT empirical literature is on public employees. The lack of consideration of politicians, and particularly the role that democratic politicians and elected governments might play in discerning the public interest, is significant. The public interest, and public values, are inherently political concepts. To simply ignore the role that politicians might play in scoping, defining, articulating the public interest and public values undermines the plausibility of PSMT. To argue – as some PSMT authors do – that public employees have a better understanding of the public interest than elected governments really does need a more developed and detailed explanation than is currently provided for in PSMT.

Second, while there is some recognition in the PSMT literature that there are different publics and different interests, there is little discussion about the implications of this for public employees wishing to further the public interest. Might different employees be motivated by different understandings of the public interest? Could different public interests lead to conflict about which interest or interests should be pursued? The public interest is not an objective truth; it is subjective, contested, multifaceted and relative. In most areas of public policy, there is not a single discernible policy option that is in the public interest; rather, there are competing policy options available, with differing public interest narratives and effects.

Nor is there a simple dichotomy between what is in the public interest, and what is not. A course of action might be both in the public and in the self-interest of the individual concerned. Perry and Wise (1990) recognise that the rational motive with public service motivation might lead employees to favour specific policies or programmes, but they do not link this to how public employees might understand the public interest.

Finally, the vagueness of what constitutes the public, publicness and the public interest raises significant questions about whether public service motivation research can determine the motives of public employees. Motivation is intangible and cannot be directly observed (Brewer, 2019). It is implied. It is challenging to understand the mix of motives that might generate specific behavioural and policy outcomes. The vagueness of the concept of the public interest within PSMT only makes this task more difficult.

Perhaps there is an alternative explanation. Maybe furthering the public interest is not important to public employees, but rather what is important is confirming an identity that involves furthering the public interest. Maybe there is utility gain from having this identity confirmed, by the individual employee and by those with whom she works and engages. If this is the case, there is no need for public employees to be able to discern the public will; no need for an understanding of whether and how they might further the public interest. There is simply expressive utility from being perceived as doing so. This is the argument I put forward in the second half of this book.

FOUR

Decision-making in public service motivation theory

Introduction

A theory of motivation is a helpful start. But public servants make decisions – about 'who gets what, when, how' (Lasswell, 1936), and they take action. Their decisions affect whether and what public services are available, who can access these services, whether some are excluded from services. They make individual decisions, and they make collective decisions. Thus, for many public policy and public administration scholars, it is not just the motivations of public servants that are of interest, but 'the decisions that public services make, how they are made, by whom and to what end, that is of primary interest' (O'Leary, 2019). Or, as Glendon Schubert (1957) argued, 'a theory of "the public interest" in administrative decision-making ought, one supposes, to describe a relationship between a concept of the public interest and official behaviour' (p 346).

In this chapter, consideration is given to how PSMT deals with administrative decision-making; with how public employees put their public service motivation into practice in their work. The chapter explores how PSMT explains (or does not discuss) the causal relationship between motivation and behaviour, and how it discusses the individual and collective behaviours of public servants. To do so, the analysis set out in this chapter focuses on the attraction to policy making domain within PSMT. Specifically, a comparison is made between how PSMT treats behaviour and decision-making that is motivated by an attraction to policy making, and how this is explained in the key Public Choice model, the bureau-shaping thesis (Dunleavy, 1991).

Behaviour and decision-making in public service motivation theory

As Carina Schott and colleagues (2018) make clear, working in the public sector involves making difficult decisions, often when facing significant dilemmas. The behaviour of public employees, how they make such decisions and what effect their levels of public service motivation have on how and what decisions they make, are therefore fundamental questions.

PSMT is about individual motivation, the 'forces that energize, direct, and sustain behaviour' (Perry and Porter, 1982); that determine the 'form, direction, intensity, and duration' of behaviour and action (Horton, 2008). Much PSMT empirical work focuses on the behaviours and behavioural outcomes of public employees, and how levels of public service motivation affect these. Several chapters in the seminal PSMT book, *Motivation in public management* (Perry and Hondeghem, 2008) discuss the behaviours associated with public service-motivated public employees. Gene Brewer (2008) states that there is a compelling argument about the link between public service motivation and individual and organisational performance, arguing that there is a range of behavioural outcomes associated with public service motivation. Brewer lists these as 'choosing public service-orientated employment, increased job involvement, and organizational commitment, and ultimately higher performance' (p 136). He goes on to consider the empirical evidence supporting these arguments.

Maesschalck and colleagues (2008) consider the relationship between ethical conduct and public service motivation. They cite previous empirical research by one of the authors that link this behaviour with public values, arguing that these 'work' values 'could easily be translated as "public service motivation values"' (p 161) and relate to conduct in public service. Finally, David Houston (2008), in a chapter entitled 'behavior in the public square', argues that the 'significance of public service motivation lies in its implications for behavior' (p 178), and argues that PSMT directly links motivation with the behaviour of public employees.

The link between levels of public service motivation and individual and organisational performance is a core area of empirical study for PSMT. From its earliest days, it has been assumed that higher levels of public service motivation are related to organisational and individual performance (Perry and Wise, 1990). Lotte Andersen and colleagues (2013) identify ten studies that evidence a positive relationship between public service motivation and individual performance. They argue that these studies show that individuals with higher levels of public service motivation tend to have higher levels of performance, although they identify the limitations of these studies, which rely on self-reporting of performance levels.

PSMT has also linked public service motivation with a number of organisation-level behaviours, including organisational citizenship behaviour (OCB), whistle-blowing and other forms of prosocial rule breaking. Typically, these are framed as positive and prosocial behaviours, although it is increasingly recognised that there might be a 'dark side' of public service motivation (Giauque et al, 2012; Brewer, 2019).

But the gap here is around collective decision-making, around policy decisions, recommendations made to ministers, what and how public services are delivered, around eligibility criteria for public services and around a whole gambit of collective decisions made by government employees every day of their working lives. This is a significant gap that has a number of dimensions, three of which are discussed here.

First, public service motivation is a multifaceted construct, consisting of different types of motivators – rational, normative and affective (Perry and Wise, 1990).These motivators are distinct. They are measured and should be considered separately, as they may have different causes and different consequences (Perry, 1996). The different motivators could be related to various public values, and might energise different behaviours, suggesting that public service-motivated individuals trade off between different values and motivators. How do they do this, and what are the implications of this when they do?

Second, public service motivation is not the only prosocial motivator that will energise and direct public employees' behaviour (Anderfuhren-Biget et al, 2014; Jensen and Andersen, 2015). Indeed, there is still some debate in the PSMT literature around whether prosocial behaviour and public service motivation are distinct concepts. Nor is it the only type of motivator (Wise, 2000). Public employees, like everyone else, have mixed and sometimes competing motives. Their behaviours and actions are also affected by factors other than their individual motivation. These factors include the type of agency they work in, its form and function, context, as well as their role within the organisation. This means that individual public employees – even with similar levels of public service motivation and facing similar contexts – might make different decisions.

Third, public employees make individual decisions, but they also make collective ones. They collaborate, negotiate and compromise when making these collective decisions. These decisions involve others from within the same profession, government agency or department. They often involve working with public employees from different professions, agencies, or departments, and with politicians.

The rest of this chapter explores these issues, examining them specifically in relation to the attraction to policy making domain. In doing so, the analysis set out here compares and contrasts how PSMT examines attraction to policy making with a Public Choice approach, Patrick Dunleavy's bureau-shaping model (Dunleavy, 1991).

Attraction to policy making and public service motivation

The attraction to policy making domain is perhaps the most controversial within PSMT. Policy making was included as the rational motive within the original Perry and Wise (1990) conception of public service motivation. Arguing that individuals might be attracted to public service to participate in policy formation and thereby meet 'personal needs while serving social interests' (p 368), including reinforcing a positive image of their own importance. The authors went on to state that rational motives might also involve promoting special interests. It can also include engaging in political forums (Andersen et al, 2013), supporting a specific policy or programme (Caillier, 2017), and 'signing initiatives, petitions and referenda, participation in demonstrations, being elected for a political mandate or membership of political organizations' (Ritz et al, 2020).

Attraction to policy making was included in Perry's measurement scale; as originally proposed, it included five statements, which included three reversed (negative) statements, of which two were about politics. It is interesting that the only two statements about politics in Perry's 24-item scale are negatively framed. It has been suggested that this latter issue might mean that empirical results could reflect dissatisfaction with politicians rather than be a comment on policy making (Coursey et al, 2008; Lee et al, 2020).

But there is ongoing debate within PSMT around whether this domain is consistent with public service motivation. On one side of this debate are those who argue that public service motivation involves a mix of motives, and this includes rational motives. They also argue that engagement in public policy is a unique feature of public employment, and often involves working closely with politicians (another unique feature of government). (See, for example, Ritz (2011).) In contrast, others argue that rational motives are inconsistent with public service motivation, because they are grounded in self-interest rather than the public interest. Several authors claim that rational motives are theoretically and empirically different to other motivational domains within public service motivation (see, for example, Kim and Vandenabeele, 2010; Kim, 2013). Underlying this side of the debate again is the assumption that rationality means individual, instrumental and selfish behaviour.

Attraction to policy making and Public Choice

It is here that I want to bring in Patrick Dunleavy's bureau-shaping thesis, as developed in his book, *Democracy, bureaucracy and public choice* (1991). Despite being published at around the same time as *The motivational bases of public service*, it is Niskanen and Downs, rather than Dunleavy's work, which is referred to in discussion of Public Choice theory and its views on the motives of public employees.

This lack of consideration is surprising. Core to Dunleavy's thesis is that public servants are motivated by an *attraction to public policy making*, and this motivation leads to bureau-shaping behaviours. In his work, Dunleavy sets out not only a theory of motivation of public employees, but also a model of how this motivation affects their collective action and decision-making, and in turn how this affects public sector reform. But it is also surprising because of the empirical work of Oliver James (2003), who compares public interest and bureau-shaping explanations of the Next Steps civil service reforms in the UK in the 1980s. These reforms are associated with NPM, not least because they were consistent with the disaggregation of units in the public sector, which is one of Christopher Hood's seven doctrines of NPM (Hood, 1991). And, like Dunleavy's thesis, the work of Oliver James is almost completely ignored by PSMT.

Dunleavy starts by widening the utility function of civil servants to include a range of intrinsic and non-pecuniary motives, primarily around policy making. He then suggests that civil servants, as rational actors, will seek to maximise their utility to shape their bureau (agency, department, ministry) so that they can focus more on policy work and being closer to political decision-making.

Dunleavy makes three insights into how rational civil servants will seek to achieve these goals.

First, he suggests that civil servants will pursue individual or collective action, depending on which they feel is more likely to succeed. Collective action here implies strategic negotiation between actors to decide the most appropriate and acceptable means of achieving collective goals, subject to any free-rider problems. But it also suggests differences by rank; senior civil servants are much more likely to focus on shaping their agencies to focus on policy work than junior civil servants, who will have less power to achieve these goals and are likely to be more interested in higher pay.

Second, Dunleavy recognises that public sector organisations are not all the same; the departments, ministries and agencies vary in terms of the type of work that civil servants do, how their funding is spent, and the form and function of their organisations. These differences create different incentives and constraints for civil servants as they try to increase their policy-focused and politician-facing work, and to decrease their routine management tasks. He identifies five basic types of government agency: (a) delivery agencies; (b) transfer agencies, which handle transfer payments (benefits, for example) from government to citizens or firms; (c) contract agencies, which manage research and development, building or service contracts; (d) control agencies, which manage funding grants to other government agencies and parts of the public sector; and (e) regulatory agencies.

These different agency types will also vary in terms of the composition of their budgets. Dunleavy identifies four budget types. Core budget (CB) represents the money spent on the agency's own operations, on staffing, accommodation and office costs. Bureau Budget (BB) includes the core budget plus any money spent on services contracted out to the private sector. Programme Budget (PB) includes the bureau budget, plus any funds transferred to other public sector organisations. Finally, Super Programme Budget (SPB) covers all of the above, plus any spending by other public sector organisations from their own resources, over which the agency has some control. Different agency types will have a different 'mix' of these four budget types.

Given these differences (in rank, in individual versus collective action, in budget composition, in agency type), Dunleavy identifies five different strategies that rational civil servants might pursue, which range from budget maximisation through to bureau-shaping.

While the bureau-shaping thesis shares some core assumptions about PSMT in terms of attraction to policy making, there are some key differences. It is these differences that provide a critique of PSMT around the link between motivation and behaviour. Table 4.1 compares the insights of the bureau-shaping thesis and the attraction to policy making domain of PSMT. The three critical differences are: (a) bureau-shaping includes a clear and testable link between motivation, behaviour and decision-making, whereas PSMT does not (O'Leary, 2015); (b) bureau-shaping recognises that the public sector is not a single, homogenous entity, and that differences between the form and function of government departments and agencies will incentivise and constrain civil servants in different ways, whereas PSMT does not; and (c) bureau-shaping provides an insight into how the decisions of civil servants can affect the size, structure and function of government departments and agencies, whereas PSMT does not.

Both bureau-shaping and the attraction to policy making domain within PSMT see public servants as being motivated by policy work. In bureau-shaping, this is the intrinsic motivation

Table 4.1: Comparison of bureau-shaping and public service motivation assumptions

	Bureau-shaping	PSMT (APM)
Motivation	Rational. Extrinsic and intrinsic. Closeness to power, policy making, status	Rational. Extrinsic and intrinsic. Policy making, status, special interests, public interest
Policy domain	Not relevant	Ignored
Politicians	Ignored or seen as exogenous	Ignored or seen as exogenous
Public employees	Yes	Contested
Public	Ignored or seen as exogenous	Ignored or seen as exogenous
Institutional design	Different and directly affects behavioural outcomes	Recognised but under theorized
Decision making	Rational. Individual and collective	Not explained
Behavioural consequences	Five different bureau-shaping behaviours	Individual level outcomes Organisational performance

of being involved in policy making, being close to power, as well as extrinsic rewards such as having status and being seen to be important. Although Dunleavy does not mention the public interest as being a motivator, I would argue that it should be included, in line with the expectations of both Anthony Downs (1967) and William Niskanen (1971). Both Downs and Niskanen make clear that public servants might be motivated to further what they perceive to be the public interest. This is a rational, other regarding motivation, entirely consistent with several Public Choice models of bureaucracy.

As discussed in Chapter Two, the role of intrinsic motivation is contested by a small number of PSMT scholars. The attraction to policy making domain also includes the extrinsic motivation of policy work (to further the public interest), furthering special interests, and also the status that such work brings. In both bureau-shaping and PSMT, the type or area of policy work undertaken is not discussed or considered important – both theories are indifferent as to whether civil servants are attracted to defence policy as to climate change policy (for further discussion about this in relation to PSMT, see Gailmard (2010)).

Both attraction to policy making and the bureau-shaping thesis largely ignore the role of politicians (although James' development of bureau-shaping theory does take into account the role of politicians). Given the rationality assumptions underpinning the bureau-shaping thesis, it would be reasonable to conclude that politicians' motivations are also rational (symmetry assumption). But as established in Chapter Two, there is some evidence to suggest that PSMT also assumes that politicians are rational and self-interested, and as such are different to public servants. More significantly, PSMT does not provide an explanation for this asymmetry in its assumptions between different types of public servants, which is a significant gap in the field. It is simply not plausible to assume that politicians are somehow different to others who serve the public good.

But the real insight, the real challenge that the bureau-shaping thesis provides to PSMT, is in its insights into the actual behaviour and decision-making of civil servants with respect to core NPM reforms. Because, contrary to the implicit assumptions of PSMT, the empirical bureau-shaping evidence suggests that it was civil servants, not politicians, that may have actively pursued these reforms in order to bureau-shape.

These insights come from three empirical research projects. Although this is much too small a body of evidence from which to draw any significant conclusions (and indeed the overall body of work on bureau-shaping is very small compared to that on public service motivation), it does raise some significant questions. For each of the three examples focuses on the observed collective behaviour of civil servants, rather than asking civil servants about their motivations (as is the case with most research in PSMT).

Robert Shaw's research focuses on departmental changes in New Zealand in the later 1990s in relation to new unemployment benefits. By analysing policy documents and changes in public budgets, he draws conclusions that bureau-shaping explains the actions of some of the senior civil servants involved in the reforms (Shaw, 2004). These reforms led to significant changes in departmental size and responsibilities, consistent with the 'disaggregation' doctrine underpinning NPM reforms. Shaw's research thus challenges the PSMT narrative that NPM reforms were imposed on civil servants by their political masters.

In an article published in 2009 by Bhatti and colleagues, the authors challenged the assumption that senior civil servants would be against the outsourcing of government services. In line with bureau-shaping expectations, the authors argue that some senior civil servants would favour outsourcing, both because the policy and commissioning work in designing and managing the contracts would be intrinsically rewarding, but also to avoid the routine management of the services being delivered. They found some evidence to support the expectations of the bureau-shaping thesis.

But it is probably the work of Oliver James in relation to the Next Steps agencies in the UK that provides the greatest challenge. The Next Steps agencies were a series of civil service reform enacted from 1988. This was a significant reform programme, which involved creating new 'executive agencies' – separate from government departments but still accountable to them – to deliver key public services. This programme of reform involved separating the policy making and ministerial support functions of the civil service from the executive and service delivery functions. These latter functions were transferred to new 'executive' agencies. These were headed by chief executives, with greater financial and managerial freedoms, and given performance targets to meet. Around three quarters of the civil service were transferred to these new executive agencies, of which over a hundred were created by the end of the last century.

These reforms were 'a key part of "New Public Management" (NPM) reform to public services' (James, 2003: 1), entirely consistent with Hood's (1991) disaggregation doctrine, and often involving reforms that were consistent with other doctrines, including hands-on professional management, explicit standards and measures of performance, and greater emphasis on output controls. The Next Steps agencies were exactly the kind of NPM reforms that should demotivate public servants, according to PSMT. The reforms contain several elements that are the antithesis of the vision for the public service that is inherent in the normative vision of PSMT. A focus on outputs and performance targets are the kind of externally imposed extrinsic motivators and are the opposite of the public management approaches that PSMT predicts will motivate staff, improve job satisfaction and improve organisational performance.

And yet, Oliver James found that it was senior civil servants – not politicians – who planned these reforms. The Next Steps proposals were 'influenced by senior officials' preferences for the organization of their departments' (p 127).

That is not to say that politicians did not play a role. Indeed, several academics have suggested that Margaret Thatcher, then prime minister, played a significant role in these reforms. Shortly after the 1979 General Election and her becoming prime minister, Mrs Thatcher appointed Sir Derek Rayner, then chief executive of Marks and Spencer, to undertake a number of inquiries into the operation and effectiveness of several parts of the civil service. In these reviews, Sir Derek was assisted and supported by officials from the civil service department, and from civil servants across government. In

Improving Management in Government: The Next Steps he set out a number of recommendations for civil service reform and for the creation of executive agencies. Although Margaret Thatcher advised Parliament that the government had accepted these recommendations, there is no evidence to suggest that she played a pivotal role in proposing them. She made no conference or other speech about the reforms, and the reforms were barely mentioned in her autobiography. Indeed, Dowding and James (2004) conclude that if 'politicians saw their role as significant, they certainly do not seem to advertise the fact' (p 184).

What might explain this? James found that senior civil servants were motived by both self-regarding and public interest considerations. He states:

> Senior officials did not seem to be pursuing exclusively self-regarding motivations in this context but a mixture of interests in their work and a view that this was the best way to make policy. Their actions were generally consistent with maintaining their position as the key policy workers in central government. (p 128)

Thus, civil servants actively pursued NPM public sector reforms, both to further their own self-interests (including the intrinsic value from doing policy work, which they enjoyed), and because they believed it was in the public interest. These findings are consistent with Public Choice understandings of the motivations of public servants, and consistent with Public Choice expectations of how those motivations (preferences, in Public Choice terminology) resulted in decisions and actions. While PSMT can provide a partial explanation for the motivations of these civil servants, it does not provide a theoretical basis for understanding the role that these motivations played in decision–making or behaviour. And this is a significant gap.

Conclusion

How do the motives of public servants affect their collective decision-making? This key question is fundamental to our understanding of public administration, yet I argue that it is largely ignored in the PSMT literature.

Motives drive behaviour. But in making behavioural decisions, public servants' actions are also influenced by the institutional design features of the public organisations in which they work. These features include the organisation's mission and objectives, its version of the public interest norm, its publicness, its closeness to specific beneficiaries, and its form and function. Although PSMT increasingly acknowledges the institutional context within which public servants operate, most empirical research still treats the public sector as a single, homogenous entity.

Public employees also make collective decisions. They barter, negotiate, compromise, collaborate, work together. It is these collective decisions that by and large effect the types of public policies that are implemented, maintained or terminated, the organisational structure of government, and the form and function of public services. They determine the eligibility criteria for accessing public services, as well as how public services are delivered, monitored and regulated. The motivations of individual public employees are only one part of the mix of preferences, context, incentives, constraints and options that affect these collective decisions. These decisions affect whether, how and to what extent the public interest is furthered by the work of public employees.

Yet it is not these outcomes that are examined in the PSMT literature. Empirical research in the field is focused on behavioural outcomes such as job satisfaction, performance, leadership, and selection and recruitment. These are, of course, important outcomes. But what is needed is more research to demonstrate whether and in what ways public service motivation furthers the public interest.

FIVE

Observing public service motivation

Introduction

The extant literature around public service motivation is overwhelmingly empirical, and usually quantitative in nature. This is a positive of PSMT, and means that there is considerable evidence to support the view that public employees have other regarding motivations.

But there are also significant issues with this empirical evidence; with its areas of focus and with the methods used. This chapter will critically explore the empirical evidence around public service motivation. It starts by examining a cohort of 52 studies, published in 2020, which include 'public service motivation' in their title. As with the overall body of research in the field, the 2020 cohort is overwhelmingly empirical in nature, and mostly uses quantitative methods.

The second half of the chapter will draw out the key criticisms and proposals for developing the research agenda around public service motivation identified by PSMT scholars themselves. These criticisms will be explored, and the 2020 cohort assessed as to the extent to which it shows progress towards addressing these criticisms.

The analysis here will conclude that empirical evidence around public service motivation continues to demonstrate methodological weaknesses. In particular, the continuing use of cross-sectional surveys and self-reported measures limits significantly the conclusions that can be drawn from the research. To some extent, the criticism here is a little harsh – much social science research uses similar methods, which often leads to more robust methods becoming feasible. It is also worth stating again that motivation cannot be directly observed, but rather must be implied. But, it is hardly surprising that, when asked, civil servants do indeed state that they are motivated by the public interest. Research that goes further than this, that asks what this means and explores the consequences of this, is needed.

Recent literature

In 2020, 52 articles were published with 'public service motivation' in the title. Details of these articles are set out in the Appendix, and were identified through a search conducted via Web of Science in January 2021. These articles represent around a third of all of the PSMT articles published in 2020. They suggest little progress has been made within the field to address some of the substantive criticisms of its research design and methods. Many of these criticisms – the reliance on cross-sectional survey data, on self-reported motivation and behaviours, the focus on public employees – come from within the field. As such, these criticisms are intended to widen and deepen our understanding of public service motivation, and to improve the robustness of this empirical work.

Each of these criticisms will be addressed and further criticisms added in the second half of this chapter. But first, I want to explore the extant empirical literature and what it says about the current state of PSMT research.

Of the 52 articles, 46 were empirical. Of these, 41 were quantitative papers, of which four used secondary data and the remainder drew on original survey data. Almost all sampled public employees as respondents. Seven covered student respondents, seven covered respondents from the general population, and one covered not-for-profit board members. None of the papers examined public service motivation in the private sector.

Thirty-six of the articles were in journals that published more than one article on public service motivation in 2020. Figure 5.1 provides counts of the number of articles published by journal (excluding journals with a single article published).

Overwhelmingly, most articles published in 2020 were in public administration or public management journals. Figure 5.2 gives an insight into the distribution of the populations sampled by region, including a split between quantitative and qualitative studies.

So far, this analysis is consistent with that provided (much more systematically and in greater depth, and using a different method) by Adrian Ritz and colleagues in their 2016 article 'Public service motivation: a systematic literature review and outlook' (Ritz et al, 2016). Ritz and colleagues included 323 articles in their final analysis. These were mostly published in public administration journals, with *Public Administration Review*, *Journal of Public Administration Research and Theory*, *Review of Public Personnel Administration*, and the *International Public Management Journal* having the highest number of published articles. Ritz and colleagues also found that most of these publications were empirical, focusing on quantitative methods using survey data and secondary analysis of survey data. Many of the studies relied on cross-sectional designs.

My analysis of the 2020 cohort of publications identifies that the largest number of studies covered respondents from North America (all from the United States). Two papers – Pautz and Vogel (2020), and Prysmakova (2020) – did not state where their respondents were located, but the language used in the articles suggests both were in the US. Bromberg and Charbonneau (2020) recruited participants from the membership of the International Public Management

Figure 5.1: Count of articles published by journal in 2020 (n=36/52)

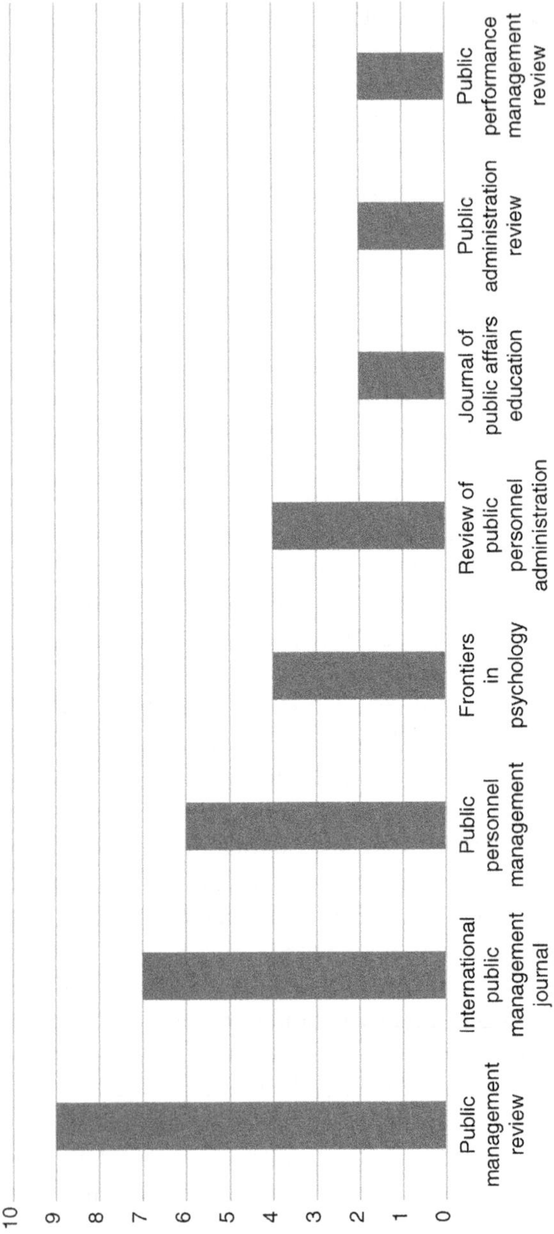

Figure 5.2: Number of articles by region, and whether quantitative or qualitative in design

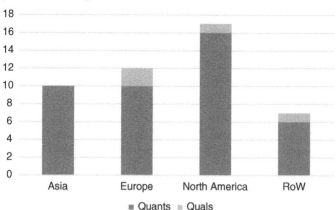

Association for Human Resources; despite its name, its membership is overwhelmingly from the US, and this has been included in the North America column.

Several of the Europe-based studies covered more than one European country. One of these (Sulkowski et al, 2020) was a qualitative piece of research of 17 staff members from three universities in Poland and Malta. The authors state that this was a convenience sample, and that there was a sufficient level of homogeneity between the universities. The authors recognise that there might be some limitations in their research design. Three of the European studies focused on police officers (not investigated in any of the other regions), and four sample students (out of seven studies in total).

Outside of Asia, Europe and North America, studies covered populations in India, Iraq and Israel, Morocco and Russia. Two were international and covered several countries.

Almost all of the empirical papers focused on the consequences of public service motivation, or where it was expected to have a moderating effect. Eleven of the papers examined the relationship between public service motivation and other prosocial behaviours, including organisational citizenship behaviour (n=4), whistle-blowing (n=2), and political participation (n=2). Other consequences of public service behaviour covered by the papers included job satisfaction, performance, leadership, and selection and recruitment. A small number examined ways of increasing the levels of public sector motivation among public employees.

Eight studies use secondary data. Most of these are from the United States, with one from Korea (Kim, 2020), and one from Switzerland (Ritz et al, 2020). The Korean study by Sangmook Kim is the only longitudinal piece of research published in 2020. It is also the only study that uses secondary data to explore the antecedents of public service motivation.

So what does this tell us about the current state of empirical research around public service motivation?

In 2014, James Perry suggested that research on public service motivation has gone through three waves. He described these as: (a) definition and measurement; (b) assessing and confirming construct validity; and (c) learning from past research and filling shortcomings and gaps (Perry, 2014). He asserted that the second wave was based on research conducted in the first decade of the 21st century, and stated that the aim of the article was to 'articulate an agenda for research during the third wave in which the field is now situated' (p 34).

There is little from the 52 articles discussed in this chapter to suggest that PSMT research is in this third wave. Many of the criticisms of empirical research in the field are still very much evident in these articles. Most of the proposals for further developing and improving the research agenda around public service motivation appear to have been ignored. Of course, it is entirely plausible that these 52 articles are not representative of the wider body of PSMT work published in 2020, or that 2020 itself was an unusual year, outwith developments in the field in the previous decade. But while this is plausible, I do not think it probable. There are several core PSMT authors represented in this literature from 2020, and the articles included here are likely to be the best in the field.

Criticisms and missed opportunities

The conceptual issues with public service motivation have been set out in Chapters Two, Three and Four. These chapters focused on key questions and issues that appear time and again in the literature. Is it inherent to public services, or can public service motivation be found regardless of setting? Does it include rational motives, and intrinsic motives? How is it different to other related concepts, such as altruism and prosocial motivation? Is it a mixture of motives, or essentially about the public interest? If it is about the public interest, what does this mean, and how do public service-motivated individuals go about furthering it? And how does public service motivation affect behaviour? These fundamental questions remain unanswered, and some still generate debate within the field.

But over and above these conceptual issues, there are also significant criticisms of the empirical evidence and the conclusions drawn from this empirical evidence. These criticisms are not, typically, from those who propose alternative motivations for public employees (exceptions being Bozeman and Su, 2015; Prebble, 2016; O'Leary, 2019). Rather, they can be found in several articles by PSMT scholars themselves, from authors including Bradley Wright and Adam Grant (2010); Perry, Hondeghem and Wise (2010); James Perry (2014); and Adrian Ritz, Gene Brewer and Oliver Neumann (Ritz et al, 2016).

Self-reported measures

Should we really be surprised that, when asked, civil servants do indeed state that they work to further the public interest? That when asked, they in fact do state that this is related to, for example, their self-reported performance? After all, the public interest is the dominant language of government, of politicians, civil servants and lobbyists. Arguably, it is important for public employees to be seen to be working to further the public interest. That there might be a social desirability bias is recognised by many in the field. Social desirability bias is a respondent's tendency to refer to themselves in a positive way, particularly with reference to relevant social norms. It is a well-known issue when self-reported measures are used.

As discussed in Chapter Two, much of the existing empirical research on public service motivation looks at public sector professionals. A defining characteristic of many professionals is a public interest norm. That is, professionals working in the public sector face two public interest norms; from working in the public sector, and working within a profession. This provides a significant risk that respondents in public service motivation studies will give socially desirable answers, and the potential for these when aggregated to lead to systemic errors that overstate levels of public service motivation. It is also the case that much of the PSMT empirical literature includes self-reporting independent and dependent variables, both of which are likely to be affected by social desirability bias.

The potential for social desirability bias has been raised within the field for some time. In two articles published in 2016, Seung Hyun Kim and Sangmook Kim discuss and test social desirability bias in relation to public service motivation. They find clear evidence of social desirability bias, particularly in relation to those antecedent characteristics which are often associated with higher levels of self-reported public service motivation (Kim and Kim, 2016a; 2016b). But there are two further studies that demonstrate the reality of this bias. One by Anne Fennimore in *Public Personnel Management* journal, and the other by Sahar Awan and colleagues in *Public Administration*.

Fennimore (2021) reports on two studies that examined communal narcissists. These are individuals who present and reference themselves as being compassionate altruists serving the public interest, as a means of hiding the fact that they are engaging in self-serving behaviour. Fennimore talks about communal narcissists wearing the cloak of moral piety, as being a saint-type bias and self-proclaimed other regarding motives. She demonstrates the relationship between public service motivation and community narcissism. While she does not discuss the potential for social desirability bias affecting her results, the potential here is clear.

Awan and colleagues' report (2020) is even more interesting. They conducted two studies – one using observational data, and one using self-reported measures. Both studies drew on the same sample population, and related to the same prosocial behaviour, and found evidence of social desirability bias.

Eight of the 2020 cohort of studies reference social desirability bias. Of those that reference social desirability bias, four studies set out how they have accounted for this, usually by making clear that the survey is completed anonymously, and four refer to the potential bias as a limitation. Thirty-four empirical studies do not mention this bias. Although a small number of these include an experimental element, at least 30 include self-reported dependent and independent variables, without explicit recognition of the potential bias in the findings, and without stating mitigation or method to reduce such bias.

Much social science research faces this issue, and it is difficult to see how motivation might be directly observed. This is to say, using self-reported measures is largely unavoidable. And it could be that the obviousness of social desirability bias in this approach is so clear that authors do not feel it necessary to explicitly raise this when reporting research. However, widening the methods used to include more experimental approaches, mixed methods and qualitative methods might help us better understand and explain the findings set out in the extant empirical research.

Cross-sectional surveys

Bradley Wright (2008), Bozeman and Su (2015) and Adrian Ritz and colleagues (2016) note the over-reliance on cross-sectional surveys in empirical research around public service motivation. These types of studies provide a snapshot at a single point of time, of measures (in this case, usually all self-reported) of variables of interest. They are often used to measure the prevalence of the concept of interest, and associated factors. Cross-sectional surveys are useful in many circumstances, and have a number of benefits. They are less expensive and more rapidly produced compared to other types of population surveys. Such studies can provide invaluable insight, including deep descriptive accounts of the population of interest. They also provide a basis from which more robust methods might be used.

But cross-sectional surveys also have a number of limitations. There is a significant potential of selection bias. There is a limited generalisability of findings. The temporal relationship between different variables cannot be determined, nor can the causal relationship. It is worth thinking through some of these limitations and what they may mean for the published PSMT literature.

One of the assumptions underpinning much of the PSMT research is that individuals with higher levels of public service motivation are more likely to work in the public sector. There are a small number of studies that make such comparisons, using cross-sectional survey data. Some have found this to be the case, others have not. Of course, there are issues with the assumption that measures used have the same meaning, are understood in the same way, and are measuring the same things across sectors (McCarthy et al, 2021), and these issues may affect the findings in these studies. But what is relevant here is that the reliance on cross-sectional surveys means that there are several questions that PSMT research cannot answer about this relationship.

For one, to what extent have public sector employees with less public interested views decided to leave the public sector before these surveys were undertaken? Or (because we have little evidence about whether and how levels of public service motivation change over time), what effect might a period of demotivation have on retention in the public sector? More significantly, just because public employees self-report higher levels of public service motivation compared to their private sector counterparts, this does not mean that this is a consequence of their place of work. How do levels of public sector motivation change over time as individuals become normalised into their public sector employment?

Take for example the relationship between public service motivation and volunteering. There are a number of studies that identify a relationship between these two variables. Several studies find that volunteering rates are higher among public sector employees than their private sector counterparts. Some of these studies are identified by Jaclyn Piatak and Stephen Holt in their recent article on prosocial behaviours and public service motivation (2020b). In doing so, these studies often appear to assert that volunteering is a prosocial behaviour that is an outcome of public service motivation, for example Kim (2020), and because public sector employees have higher levels of public service motivation, they are more likely to engage in other prosocial behaviours such as volunteering.

But there are a number of problems with these claims. First, as Piatak and Holt point out, many of these studies use sector of employment as a proxy for public service motivation. Basically, they assume that public sector employees will have higher levels of public service motivation and, when they find that public sector employees report higher levels of volunteering, they conclude that this is related to levels of public service motivation. These are quite heroic assumptions to make, particularly as the cross-sectional nature of much of the underlying data means that such causal inferences cannot be made.

But it is also problematic because we know that previous experience of volunteering is predictive of future volunteering (Dawson et al, 2019). We also know that opportunities for, and exposure to, volunteering are important predictors of volunteering (Ertas, 2020). And, it is also the case that an individual's prosocial behaviour can be dependent on the prosocial behaviour of others around them (Awan et al, 2020). Given that public sector and third sector organisations are more likely to provide such exposure and opportunities, it is plausible to assume that there would be higher rates of volunteering among public sector and third sector employees.

It is also the case that much of the PSMT research focuses on professionals; professionals who will have had considerable opportunity to volunteer during their university studies. And because the cross-sectional nature of much PSMT research only provides a snapshot at a single point in time, it is not possible to examine how volunteering rates in public sector employees might change over time, and whether there were any previous experiences of volunteering before entering public employment.

Thirty-three of the 2020 cohort of studies use primary, cross-sectional survey data. (n=33/42 quantitative empirical studies, just under 80 per cent.) This is consistent with the significant body of quantitative, empirical research around public service motivation (Ritz et al, 2016). While this cohort does include one longitudinal study (Kim, 2020), and several that include experimental designs (see, for example, Bromberg and Charbonneau, 2020; Ki, 2020; Weißmüller et al, 2020), the evidence generated from these studies is overwhelmingly based on cross-sectional surveys.

The use of cross-sectional studies in public service motivation research nevertheless has many benefits. It enables comparative research, should provide an essential base from which to develop my robust and more demanding empirical studies. And, as I have previously made clear, it is one of the strengths of PSMT that it does focus on empirical research rather than endless theorising.

Public sector focus of research

As established in Chapter Two, one of the ongoing arguments within the field is the foci of public service motivation. That is, whether public service motivation is a unique feature of the public sector, or does it exist regardless of setting. While increasingly the arguments lean towards the latter, measures and empirical research on public service motivation has been dominated by research on public sector employees (Ritz et al, 2016).

There is little evidence from the 2020 cohort of studies to suggest there has been a change in this focus. Of the 46 empirical studies, not a single study focuses on private sector employees. There are seven studies that examine the general population; all but one (Ripoll and Schott, 2020) of these is from the United States, and most use secondary data for their analysis. One study (Ward and Miller-Stevens, 2020) looks at non-profit board members, and several focus on students. But otherwise, the literature continues to be dominated by research on public sector employees, and about their employment activities and behaviours.

Mixed motives

Several PSMT authors assert that public employees have mixed motives; both because public service motivation comprises a mixture of rational, normative and affective motivations, and because public service motivation is not the only motivation that public sector employees have at any given time. Indeed, several studies suggest that public service motivation might be a minor consideration in the overall motivational mix; for example, Sangmook Kim (2016) cites data suggesting that the primary motive for becoming a civil servant in Korea is consistently job security, and that other regarding motives were cited as the most important reason by under a quarter of respondents. Kim states that the third highest reason given – attractive role and sense of mission in public service – relates to public service motivation, though does not take into account the potential intrinsic nature of 'attractive role'.

Other than Kim's research, and despite the statements that public service motivation is multi-motivation, and is but one motive that drives public employees, most PSMT research focuses solely on public service motivation. Much of the research takes public service motivation to be a single, aggregate measure, rather than considering each of the four domains individually. This means that empirical research does not take account of potential conflicts between these different motivational domains. Such conflicts might arise say, for example, between the rational motive to support special interests and the normative motive to further the public interest as a whole. Or between a compassionate motive to favour a particular disadvantaged service user and the public value of equity.

The 2020 cohort very much sees public service motivation as an aggregate measure of its four domains, and does not treat them separately. Furthermore, none of this set of studies examines motives other than public service motivation.

Alternative explanations

My final criticism is the lack of a counterfactual in almost all research on public service motivation. Of course, this criticism could be levied at almost any area of research, but given the mixed findings in PSMT empirical research, the ongoing debate as to whether public service motivation is a consequence or cause of public employment, prosocial behaviour and socialisation, for example, this lack of consideration of alternative explanations is significant. It is also significant because of the ongoing debate about what exactly is public service motivation, and how is it different from other prosocial motivations and behaviours. In the 2020 cohort, only two studies – Davis et al (2020), and Potipiroon and Wongpreedee (2020) – explore potential alternative explanations.

Conclusion

Its empirical focus is undoubtedly one of the strengths of public service motivation research. Much excellent work has been done to develop valid measures of the construct, and to provide evidence about the existence of other regarding motives in public sector employees.

While this chapter has been critical of how this research has been conducted, it should also be recognised that some of the challenges set out are unavoidable. It could be argued that it is not possible to directly observe motivation, but only infer it (as several academics in the field have made clear). As such, despite their limitations, self-reported measures may be the only reasonable means by which public service motivation might be examined. Equally, while cross-sectional studies have significant limitations, their use in public service motivation research has provided an extensive and rich empirical base from which to explore and further develop the construct, and a great starting point from which to develop more robust research designs.

Yet still, some seven years after James Perry set out areas for developing public service motivation research – more robust research designs, improving measurements, research on multiple motives – it seems that little progress has been made.

PART II

Expressively motivated public employees

SIX

Rationality, expressive interests and public service motivation

Introduction

Despite the criticisms set out in the first part of this book, the argument here is not that people are motivated only for instrumentally, self-interested reasons. In our everyday lives, we often see random acts of kindness. Some people are clearly motivated to benefit others, to make a contribution to society, to make a difference to their communities. Rather, the argument put forward is that public service motivation does not provide a convincing or complete explanation for such other regarding motives observed by public employees in their work for government.

Public service motivation proposes that public employees make material sacrifices in order that they can work to further the public interest, and this is a higher order, a quality shared mostly by those 'who accept the call'. And, importantly, that this is not consistent with rational choice theory. But there is a fundamental issue that PSMT does not address. This gap – and the other issues with the theory and empirical research set out in the first part of this book – means that PSMT does not provide a satisfactory explanation of other regarding motives of public employees.

This fundamental issue is the lack of explanation of how public employees understand the public interest, understand how to further the public interest and know when they have made a contribution to the public interest. This issue is discussed in detail in Chapter Three. If the common good is so fundamentally important to public service-motivated public employees and is core to PSMT, these questions should have been addressed in the literature or be seen as important.

This chapter sets out an alternative explanation of the motivation and behaviours of public employees to the one offered by PSMT. This explanation is consistent with an understanding of human rationality and agency, but it takes a wider view of our utility function to include other regarding and expressive goals. Importantly, it addresses the fundamental issue with how public employees discern the public interest. Because it is rooted in rational choice theory, it is consistent with other middle-range theories in public policy, political science and the wider social sciences. As such, this explanation sees observed other regarding motives and behaviours as consistent with, not an alternative to, rationality.

This chapter is structured as follows.

I will first set out some core assumptions that underpin the approach taken to explain observed other regarding motivation and behaviour in public sector employees. In line with the symmetry assumption of Public Choice theory, this does not start with an assumption that public employees are somehow different to anyone else in how their motivation drives behaviour. But their preferences, and the actions they take to realise these preferences, are affected by and affect the social reality of working in the public sector.

In the second part of this chapter, I explore the concept of expressive motivation as an important part of our rational choices as human beings. The argument is that expressive motivation – of taking an action for its own sake, such as the enjoyment of the task and the sense of personal meaning it might bring, and because it reinforces how we see ourselves and how we want others to see us – is a plausible explanation of the self-reported public service motives of public employees. In doing so, the relationship between expressive motivation and (an individual actor's understanding of) the public interest; between expressive motivation and decision-making; and expressive motivation and the empirical literature around public service motivation is explored.

Assumptions

It is essential to first set out some broad assumptions about motivation and behaviour, about the public sector and about public employees. These are intended to set the framework within which the role of expressive motivation and how it affects the behaviour of public employees is discussed.

Human motivations and behaviour

The assumptions here are consistent with 'wide' versions of rational choice theory, which do not limit human motives to egotistical or instrumental goals. But they do start with an assumption that humans are rational, in that we take reasoned, goal-oriented action. These goals – our preferences, motivations, values and beliefs – are self- and other regarding. Indeed, self- and other regarding motives are not dichotomous opposites, in that *almost all human behaviour is grounded in both self- and other regarding motives.* Importantly, our self-regarding behaviour may well have other regarding outcomes, and our other regarding behaviour can also benefit us individually. Equally, we may posit our self-regarding motives as other regarding.

We are social animals, and we inhabit social contexts. As humans, we have developed a number of 'rules of the game' that help us coordinate and cooperate with each other, that incentivise and constrain our behaviour in collective action situations. These rules of the game – norms – affect and are affected by our decisions.

Although we are rational actors, not all of our actions are rationally motivated.

We are also moral and emotional actors. And as rational actors, our actions are affected by, and affect, the social contexts in which we find ourselves. This is a dynamic process. Our motives are not fixed over our lifetimes, but are adaptive. This is an important difference between standard economic theory (in which preferences are assumed to be fixed) and some wider versions of rational choice theory. The social situations in which we find ourselves may change; so that, even if our motives are the same, the behaviours driven by these motives are differently affected by changes in our social situation.

The public sector

The public sector is not a single, homogenous entity. Rather, it is a collection of departments, ministries, agencies, organisations and teams. Closeness to ministers, agency or organisational type, what is being delivered and how, all create differences between public sector organisations.

But there are some facets that are unique to, and uniquely shared by, public sector organisations. One of its most important shared and unique qualities is the norm of the public interest. While there are variations in this norm between public organisations, and how it has developed and changed over time, that there is a norm of the public interest is generally a common feature of all public sector organisations. This norm affects, and is affected by, the individual and collective decisions of public servants.

The public sector is also a political and a Political institution. Government organisations are engaged in decisions about who gets what, when, how (Lasswell, 1936). They also, uniquely, involve politicians. Government is also a monopoly, engaging in non-market and generally collective goods and services activities. A model of the motivation of public employees needs to take these factors into account.

Thus, as the behaviours of public employees are affected by, and affect, the institutional settings within which they work, it is reasonable to expect that these differences between parts of the public sector will be material. There are at least three institutional domains that are significant: (a) the degree of publicness and the extent to which there is direct political accountability for the organisation's work; (b) the form and function of the organisation; and (c) the organisation's beneficiaries, and the closeness of public employees to these beneficiaries.

In their work in public sector organisations, public employees are engaged in the delivery of collective goods and services, often involving collective action. In doing so, they barter, negotiate and compromise.

Fundamental to my argument here is that the extent to which their actions can affect public outcomes is often limited. For example, consider High Speed 2 (HS2), the UK's largest infrastructure project. This is a major railway linking several large cities in England, taking decades and many billions of pounds to complete. An individual public employee working on HS2 is unlikely to have a decisive, individual effect on the project as a whole. For many, their work on the project will be complete long before HS2 opens for passengers. It is reasonable to assume that public employees will likely take this low probability of effect into account when making decisions. This is different in nature to the effect of a clinician working in publicly funded healthcare, who might be able to assess the benefit their actions have on the health of the specific population who are beneficiaries of their clinical specialism.

Motivation and decision

Motivation is important, as it energises and directs behaviour. Motivation is the preferences we have and the goals we want to achieve. But motivation is separate from behaviour. The decisions we make and the actions we take will be driven, but not determined by, our motives. The options available to us, our reasoned consideration of those options, the context within which we find ourselves, the incentives and constraints we face, our consideration of others, our previous decisions, and our values and identity, are all important factors in our decision-making.

Expressive motivation

Rational choice theory has long acknowledged that many human behaviours are non-rational in nature. Dating back to the work of Adam Smith on moral values (Smith, 2006 [1759]), there are several areas that rational choice theory accepts are outside of its remit. Emotions, and any action taken based on emotions, is largely considered not to be rational as this does not entail reasoned choice (Elster, 2009). It is also the case that much rational choice literature makes few assumptions about what an individual's preferences might be, or from where these preferences originate. In rational choice explanations of religion (for example), faith is assumed to be a preference and thus a given. Rather than focus on this preference or its origin, rational choice theories of religion focus on decisions about how this faith is practised (see, for example, Stark and Bainbridge, 1987; Iannaccone, 1992). And until the Nobel Prize-winning work of American economist Gary Becker, the family was considered an area where rational choice theory would have no or limited explanatory power (Hechter and Kanazawa, 1997).

Since the 1960s, the focus of rational choice theories has evolved considerably. While all rational choice theories share three core assumptions (preferences affect behaviour, choices are made taking account of incentives and constraints, actors choose actions that will best satisfy their preferences), there are several different ways to describe the differences between rational choice theories. Thick and thin versions (where thin versions make no assumptions about the preferences or constraints of rational actors), and narrow and wide versions are two of the ways in which debates within rational choice theory are described.

As established in Chapter One, it is this narrow version of rational choice theory against which PSMT is posited.

Karl-Dieter Opp (1999) has identified five key differences between the narrow and wide versions of rational choice theory. The first of these relates to assumptions of preferences of rational actors; narrow versions of rational choice theory assume only egotistical preferences, whereas wider versions posit that all kinds of preferences can have explanatory power.

It is here that the concept of expressive choice should be introduced.

Rational behaviour is goal-orientated behaviour. In instrumental-only versions of rational choice, the goal is considered to be separate from the action taken to achieve that goal.

So, for example, a rational actor who wants to get from London to Glasgow (preference or goal) has three options. She can fly, she can drive, or she can take the train. In instrumental-only versions, it is assumed that she is indifferent about which of these options she takes, subject to the incentives and constraints she faces. These incentives and constraints might include the time taken by each mode of transport (one-hour flight, four and a half hours train time, eight hours drive time), and the cost of each (£60 flight, £110 by train, £60 by car).

In expressive accounts of rational choice, a rational actor's preferences or goals can also be *the same as* the actions taken to achieve these goals. Thus, this rational actor may choose to travel by train because she enjoys train travel. Her choices are then which train, how long a journey, and the such. But the preference (train to Glasgow) and the action (taking a train journey) are the same. Her action to travel by train to Glasgow has both expressive (going by train because she enjoys train journeys) and instrumental (going by train to get to Glasgow) utility. Her total utility is therefore the sum of the instrumental and expressive behaviour.

In this account, expressive choice is about intrinsic motivation (Chong, 2000; Hillman, 2010). Intrinsic motivation is important to all human activities, and it is not plausible to suggest that we are motivated solely by external incentives (Frey, 1997). Intrinsic motivation is also entirely consistent with a rationalist understanding of human behaviour.

Expressive choice is not just about intrinsic motivation. It can also be about values, and about identity. Expressive behaviour is action that enables a rational actor to confirm to herself and to others fundamental aspects of her identity and the values that are important to her. A rational actor might be motivated to express her values and beliefs, and take action that enables her to do so. All people act expressively because our identities affect our behaviours (Hillman, 2010). Expressive motivation arises because individuals want to demonstrate positive, prosocial attributes and moral values. In doing so, the rational actor might be motivated by self-approval, but also the approval of others.

Using the trip to Glasgow example again, an expressively motivated actor might take the train because it expresses her environmentalist values. The actor believes that taking the train is better in terms of carbon footprint than the two alternatives available (taking the car or flying) and therefore takes the train because it affirms her green values and identity, both to herself and to others. Her total utility therefore comprises her instrumental utility, plus the value to her of confirming her green identity and values and the intrinsic enjoyment she gains from travelling by train.

Expressive choice affects all types of political behaviour. For example, an expressively rational actor might comment on Twitter or other social media platforms not to change the minds or behaviours of other Twitter users, but rather to affirm their political identity to themselves and others. The motivation is not to affect political outcomes, but to be seen as someone who is involved politically (Schuessler, 2000).

It signals the values that the individual holds or wants to be seen to hold, to reflect a view they hold of the type of person they are, what they stand for and what is important to them. Expressive utility is gained by 'confirming pleasing attributes of being generous, cooperative, trusting and trustworthy, or ethical and moral' (Hillman, 2010). As the motivation is not to affect political outcomes, it is immaterial to the expressively rational actor whether or not they have such an effect. Such an actor is not concerned with instrumental outcomes, but rather with expressive utility gain. That is, the goal is not to change others' views, and the actor's utility is therefore not dependent on whether she could or has changed any views. Rather, the utility gain is achieved by this expressively motivated actor confirming her own identity as a politically engaged individual.

Expressive voting

That a person's values and identity may affect their rational decisions, particularly non-market decisions, is now generally accepted (see, for example, Frey, 1997, Akerlof and Kranton, 2010 and more recently, Prosser, 2020). In rational choice theory, this development began with the work of Anthony Downs, and the publication of his *Economic theory of democracy* (1997 [1957]). The book includes a number of parts that focus on the positioning of political parties and assumptions about their preferences, and a theorem on how rational actors make decisions about for whom to vote. In this account, Downs considers only instrumental explanations of why people vote, arguing that this decision is dependent upon the benefit of her preferred candidate being elected and the probability that her vote will be decisive, being greater than the cost to her of voting.

As such, a rational actor would face significant information costs in deciding which is her preferred candidate. She would need to weigh up each candidate's policy positions, assessing the likely cost or benefit to her. And, given this and the fact that the probability of her vote being decisive is extremely low (in a typical UK Parliamentary constituency, probably around 1 in 55,000), it would be irrational for an actor to vote. Of course, people do vote, and the Downsian model was therefore criticised as creating a paradox of the rational voter. The paradox arises because such an instrumental model would predict almost zero turnout, yet so many people do turn out to vote, meaning either those voters were acting irrationally or some 'other regarding' individual preferences, not accounted for in the model, were part of the rational decisions of voters.

Rational choice scholars have spent many years trying to resolve this paradox. Starting with the work of William Riker and Peter Ordeshook (1968) who sought to amend the Downsian model to account for non-instrumental motivations. While Downs had identified that some rational actors might vote because of their civil duty, it was Riker and Ordeshook who developed a model to explain this. In their thesis, some actors vote because the action of voting is itself the goal of voting, that is 'the reward, in utiles, that an individual voter receives from his [sic] act of voting' (p 25).

Thus, voters are intrinsically motivated to vote by the act of voting itself, by participating in the democratic process. The outcome of the election is not important to this rational voter's decision; it is simply taking part in the election that generates a utility gain. This has subsequently become known as expressive voting.

But while this tells us why a rational actor might vote, it does not help us understand for whom that vote would be cast.

Later developments in the model proposed that voter choice on preferred candidates was not the result of a detailed calculation of the net benefits of each candidate's policy platform, but rather an indication of expressive voters' political beliefs and political identity. Rather than being instrumentally motivated to vote for candidate x (the process of voting as a means of getting the preferred candidate elected), it becomes an expressively motivated action (voting for candidate x to express political support for candidate x).

Alexander Schuessler (2000) says that they are expressively motivated; that is, voting is a 'means of expressing political beliefs and preferences and, in doing so, to establish or reaffirm their own political identify' (p 87). It is expressively motivated because the behaviour – the expression of political values – is valuable to the individual 'in its own right' (Hamlin and Jennings, 2011: 645). As with the act of voting itself, the expressive voter is indifferent to whether their vote is decisive to the outcome of the election. Rather, the utility gain is derived from affirming political identify and supporting a preferred candidate.

One of the significant consequences of expressive motivation is that it can generate different behaviours to its equivalent instrumental motivation. Ayre Hillman (2010) provides an example of this in relation to voting. He suggests that an instrumental voter would vote for the candidate nearest to their ideal from the available candidates (utility maximisation given constraints). In contrast, an expressively motivated voter would take into consideration the distance between their political beliefs and the available candidates.

Much of the empirical work around expressive rationality is still focused on expressive voting. But expressive motivations can be the driving force behind a significant number of human behaviours, and are relevant in all organisational and institutional settings. I argue here that expressive motivation provides an alternative explanation of the motivations of public employees. It is one of a range of rational motives that directs and energises public servants, their decisions to seek and retain public employment, and in their individual and collective decisions.

The different motivations of public employees

Rationality is goal-orientated behaviour. The goal – the preferences or motivation of that behaviour – might be self- or other regarding, instrumental or expressive. Indeed, these two dimensions are not dichotomies. Many motives lie somewhere along these two continuums – self-/other regarding, instrumental/expressive. Rarely will the motives or behaviours of public employees (or anyone else) be entirely grounded in instrumental and self-regarding motivation. Nor will they be entirely expressive or other regarding. And the decisions and behaviours of public employees might be directed by a mixture of these four motivational dimensions.

Given this, individuals might be motivated to enter public service and continue to work for government for a variety of rational reasons.

Table 6.1 sets out some of the other rational motives that might be at play. I suggest in this table that rational actors might be motivated instrumentally, expressively, or a mixture of the two. They might have self- or other regarding motives, or some combination thereof. Although rational choice is often assumed only to be interested in instrumental, self-regarding motivation, as I have argued here, since the 1960s it has increasingly widened its scope to include non-instrumental and other regarding motives (O'Leary, 2019).

The concept of instrumental, self-regarding motivation is familiar enough that it needs little explanation. These types

Table 6.1: The different rational motives of public employees

	Instrumental	Expressive
Self-regarding	Job security Job satisfaction Pay and pensions Public policy making	Warm glow altruism Being a public servant Being seen to work for the public sector Confirm identity as someone who works for the public interest
Other regarding	Helping others Reciprocal altruism Furthering the public interest	Being seen to be involved in a policy area Being seen to further the public interest

of motivational goals for public employees might include job security, pay and pensions, opportunities to affect public policy in an area of personal interest or commitment, or furthering special interests of a group to which they belong or whose values and objectives they share.

Importantly, instrumental motives might be other regarding. A rational actor might choose public employment because they are motivated to make a contribution to society. They might be motivated to help others experiencing x condition or y social problem. These are instrumental because the action taken (public employment) is separate from the motivation for taking that action (helping others). And it is rational because the actor makes a reasoned choice that the best way of achieving their goal of helping others is by taking the action of public employment rather than some other behaviour.

Public service motivation as expressive motivation

Expressive motivation is different. An individual is expressively motivated to work in the public sector because the act of being a public employee itself generates utility. That is, it is a property of the act or behaviour itself that is the motivational force (Hamlin and Jennings, 2011). Why might some individuals be motivated to work in the public sector?

A person might be motivated to work in the civil service because they enjoy public policy work, or to work as a teacher because they enjoy teaching, or to work as a doctor because they enjoy practising medicine. They value the intrinsic reward that work can bring in of itself. There might also be instrumental benefits. A policy-focused civil servant may derive instrumental utility from being involved in policy work if that results in policy gains for themselves or for others, for the prestige that results from this type of activity, or from working closely with government ministers.

But a rational actor might be motivated to work in the public sector by what this says about her, about her values, what it symbolises about her identity. An expressively motivated individual wishes to communicate her values and beliefs, to affirm her identify to others and herself. In this case, she is not being motivated by the act of doing government work, but rather about what being a public servant signals about her values and identity. To use one of the two examples from earlier, this expressive motivation to be a teacher would be the professional identity of teachers, and what being a teacher conveys – both to the actor herself and to others – about her identity. She is expressing a preference in order to attach herself to the social identity associated with being a teacher. Equally, a rational actor might be motivated to become a medical doctor because of professional identity and set of values this conveys. And it is one of the interesting facets of professions that professional identity often extends well into retirement; indeed, several UK professions regulators have special registration statuses to cover this. The process of 'being' is more important than the outcomes associated with the 'doing' of the role (Schuessler, 2000).

There are several facets of expressive motivation that are important here in relation to public employees.

One of the enduring narratives of public service is that of altruism. This line of argument is that public servants have sacrificed personal gain for the higher purpose of serving the public good. As set out elsewhere in this book, several definitions of public service motivation relate it or equate it to altruism, and one of the dimensions that is common to all of the measurement instruments is that of self-sacrifice. So why would a rational actor choose an altruistic public gain over personal loss?

First, it is important to distinguish between pure altruism and warm glow altruism. Pure acts of altruism – when the individual acts to benefit others even if this involves personal costs to themselves – include an individual running into a burning building to save the life of a child who is unknown or unrelated to them. In reality, many acts of altruism also provide benefits to the individual undertaking the act. An individual who volunteers at a local charity, for example, might benefit by making new friends, feeling useful, developing new and valuable skills, as well as feeling good about the contribution they are making to their community. A public employee also benefits from their employment in terms of pay, pensions, the value of being seen to work in the public interest and because they enjoy the work.

Very few acts of public employees are ones of pure altruism. Public employees may gain a sense of meaningfulness from helping others through their roles. While many public servants do engage in altruistic acts, they are often what James Andreoni (1990) has called 'impure' altruism or warm glow altruism. Individuals experience a 'warm-glow', some personal reward which is in itself the motivation for helping others. This warm glow altruism is self-regarding and is instrumental, even though it also benefits others. Indeed, recent work by Oliver Neumann (2019) is interesting in this regard. In an examination of reciprocity norms in public service motivation, Neumann found evidence that altruism is not selfless and includes expectations of reciprocity.

But public employees are also paid for their work. The extent of their instrumental loss from undertaking these expressive actions is, in many cases, therefore limited to the difference between the salary and other benefits they get from the public employment, and the pay and rewards they may get in an alternative private sector job. And given the importance of public employment to the individual's sense of identity and meaningfulness in work, the cost of this expressive behaviour is low compared to the benefit derived from this expression. This is particularly significant for those public sector roles for which there is no real private sector equivalent.

Expressive motivation and the public interest

So far, I have suggested that furthering the public interest might be an instrumental, other regarding motivation. But the concept of the public interest is an abstract, distal and contested one, which significantly reduces the likelihood that a rational actor would instrumentally work to further it. In most cases, an individual public employee will not be able to discern whether the public interest has been furthered and, if it has, whether and what contribution she has made to this. This holds whether the public interest is objectively defined, or is an actor's perception of what is in the public interest that is important. This subjective view of the public interest is posited by Anthony Downs and William Niskanen, but also recognised within the PSMT literature (see, for example, Andersen and Serritzlew, 2012; Schott et al, 2015).

Without knowing the probability that her contribution will be decisive to any public interest outcome gain, and given the fact that the public interest is arguably a public good and thereby prone to free-rider problems, an instrumentally rational individual is unlikely to pursue action driven by this *instrumental* motive alone.

There are of course significant exceptions to this assumption. A civil servant may play a pivotal role in implementing a new programme that has a demonstrable positive effect on programme recipients and also saves money for taxpayers. In such circumstances, the civil servant may be instrumentally motivated to serve the public interest. Or, the nature of the common good produced by the programme or public service benefits a definable group of service users with whom the civil servant has a direct relationship or affinity. This might also foster instrumental other regarding behaviour. It is an area of debate within PSMT as to whether the latter is consistent with public service motivation, but it clearly produces some direct benefit to others and may well have second-order, longer-term benefits too. In such circumstances, furthering the public interest may be instrumentally rational.

But let us assume that many examples of furthering the public interest are different to the examples set out earlier. That there is no such thing as an objective, uncontested, understanding of the public interest. So that whether public sector reorganisations, advice to ministers, public policy change and implementation, changes to eligibility criteria for public programmes, and changes in funding for specific services and the such, might be seen by some to be in the public interest, and others to be decidedly against the public interest. The abstract, distal and contested nature of the public interest as a concept means that it is generally impossible to agree on whether a specific Act of Parliament, public programme, or public service did or did not contribute to the public good. And yet, many public employees state that furthering the public interest is an important motivational driver for them.

Here, I would argue that furthering the public interest is a form of expressive motivation. Because what is important is not the instrumental contribution that an individual public employee makes to the public good, but the extent to which she can claim, to herself and to others, that she has made some such contribution. She does not do x activity to produce y outcome, but rather to be seen as and to confirm her identity as an x-performer (Schuessler, 2000). This is again an important part of her identity, of undertaking acts that are symbolic of her values and beliefs.

What does this mean in terms of furthering the public interest?

An individual public employee is unlikely to be able to understand the contribution that she makes to furthering the public interest, especially where she has: (a) no direct relationship with the beneficiaries (or there are no specific beneficiaries); and (b) where the likely public interest outcome is some distance away, or in some way lacks specificity. The collective nature of furthering the public interest also means that the probability of this individual's contribution being decisive is very low. It may not, therefore, be instrumentally rational for an individual public employee to seek to further the public interest in these circumstances. In contrast, it stands to reason that where there are directly identifiable beneficiaries, and where the individual public employee can more easily discern the effect of their work on these beneficiaries, then it becomes increasing instrumentally rational for the employee to seek to further the public interest.

However, if the public employee is expressively motivated, then whatever the probability of her contribution being decisive to furthering the public interest, she will act anyway. Because for an expressively motivated public employee, it is immaterial whether she in fact furthers the public interest or whether her contribution to furthering the public interest is decisive. What is important – what she derives expressive utility from – is whether her actions confirm her values as someone who is motivated by the public interest. In this sense, her expressive behaviour is self-interested (Hamlin and Jennings, 2019).

As such, the significant gap in the PSMT literature around how public employees make decisions about what is in the public interest does not matter. In the expressive explanation of the role of the public interest in their motivation, public employees are not motivated by the instrumental goal of having a positive effect on the public interest, but rather on the expressive motivation of what working in the public sector symbolises about their public interest values and the importance of the common good to their identity.

Expressive motivation and decision-making

So far I have posited that rational public servants will be motivated to seek and retain employment in the public sector because of, at least in part, the expressive utility this brings them. This utility is derived by confirming their values and political identity, both to themselves and to others, and because they enjoy the type of work they undertake. I have also suggested that they are motivated by instrumental utility. In any given situation, purely expressive motivation is rare, and public employees are likely to be motivated by a mix of expressive and instrumental motives.

As such, a public employee's total utility is the sum of instrumental and expressive (the intrinsic reward gained from doing enjoyable work, and the extrinsic reward gained from confirming her identity).

But how does expressive motivation factor into an understanding of how public employees make decisions, either individual decisions or collective decisions? What is the link between expressive motivation and expressive behaviour? And are there any public policy consequences of this?

Public servants make decisions. They make individual decisions, and they make collective decisions. The utility derived from these decisions is the sum of their instrumental and expressive utilities. For some decisions, these two motivational bases will be complementary. In others, there will be a conflict, with different behaviours indicated by the instrumental versus the expressive motivations. In such cases, rational public employees will trade off between the two motivational drives. How these motivations drive behaviour is therefore important.

First, any individual will be motivated both instrumentality and expressively, and public servants will therefore have both types of motive. Pure cases of either instrumental or expressive motivation are unlikely, suggesting that individuals will trade off between these two when making decisions. In most general cases, expressive behaviour is considered more likely in low-cost situations. As an explanation of election behaviour, the cost of expressive voting to an individual voter is low because they do not incur any information costs in deciding between different candidates. As such, the material loss that a rational voter might incur because of their expressive behaviour is very low. In such cases, rational actors are more likely to disregard material utility in favour of expressive utility (Hillman, 2010). The argument here is that working in the public sector exhibits similar characteristics. The probability that an individual public employee's contribution to furthering the public interest is decisive is very low. The nature of public sector employment, particularly in terms of job security, the monopolistic and non-market nature of government, and because of the political accountability of politicians, is such that an individual public employee is unlikely to experience a loss of instrumental utility through their expressive behaviour.

Of course, the argument here would be that pay differentials between public sector and private sector workers are such that expressive rationality is unlikely to provide a rational reason for public sector employment.

However, this argument is not sustainable.

In the UK, public sector workers have been paid more than the private sector works over the past 25 years. Controlling for age and qualifications, between 1993 and 2020, this pay differential varied from a high of nearly 10 per cent to almost parity in 2001–02 and again in 2019–20 (Cribb et al, 2019). And, during the various lockdowns of 2020 and 2021, the gap has grown again. It is also important to note that this gap excludes pensions, and historically public sector pensions have been higher than their private sector equivalents. In the UK context at least, the PSMT claim that public sector workers are sacrificing personal gain to further the public interest simply does not stack up.

But even if there was a pay gap in favour of the private sector, expressive motivation might still provide an explanation for some individuals seeking and retaining public sector employment. An individual might accept lower-paid employment for expressive reasons; if the expressive benefit is greater than the material loss suffered. And given the importance that many public sector employees place on furthering the public interest, it is likely that this is the case for many. Indeed, I would argue that unique features of the public sector are such that the extent to which a rational individual will trade off these material losses for the expressive benefits of working for the public good will increase over time.

Institutional settings will influence the balance between instrumental and expressive motivations, and the extent to which each drives behaviour (Hillman, 2010). Institutional settings here will include the pay, reward and promotion structure, the form and function of the organisation, and any institutional norms. In most public sector organisations, pay, promotion and reward structures are fairly fixed, and individual employees cannot individually influence these. And, argued here and as is made clear in the PSMT literature, there is a strong institutional norm of furthering the public good in many public sector organisations.

Rational actors respond to norms in the same way they respond to other incentives and constraints when deciding what action to take to best achieve their goals. Norms are the means by which we internalise institutional rules of the game, enabling us to coordinate our collection behaviour and social interactions and to cooperate when in our collective interests. The public good norm that is prevalent in many public organisations will increasingly favour expressive motives the longer an individual works in the public sector, subject to differences in the form and function of the organisation. Indeed, empirical work on public service motivation confirms that it increases with tenure, suggesting that behaviour is increasingly affected as this norm becomes more important. But there is a secondary effect here that also positively favours expressive motives. Because value-expressive behaviour is relative to an audience – the rational actor is expressing and confirming her values and identity to herself and to others – she will seek out and join groups of like-minded individuals. In public sector organisations, this is a reciprocal process, as employees confirm with each other their public good values and identity. This suggests that the extent to which a rational public employee engages in expressive behaviour will be mediated by the size of the organisation in which she works, or the policy networks within with she operates.

Indeed, there is a significant difference in the collective decision-making of a purely instrumentally motivated and purely expressively motivated public employee (Hamlin and

Jennings, 2019). Collective action is joint action in pursuit of a common objective. It involves cooperation, interpersonal trust, agreement of common goals and complementary motivations. Public employees engage in collective action in a range of different situations; policy development is rarely a lone pursuit, nor is much of social service provision. Of course, much of the time this cooperation is incentivised by work roles, organisational objectives and management structures. But where such incentives do not exist or are weak, instrumental and expressive motivations are expected to lead to different behavioural outcomes in terms of collective action. (It is worth noting that there is little mention of the collective action of public employees in the PSMT literature. Behavioural outcomes considered empirically are either individual or organisational level consequences.)

Instrumentally motivated public employees are expected to face collective action problems when they try to further their common goals, especially if those goals are public goods (that is, in the economic sense, to the extent that they are non-excludable and non-rivalrous). They can resolve these collective action problems under certain circumstances, but otherwise the individually rational decision not to cooperative will lead to a sub-optimal social outcome. This classic theory of collective action problems was first set out by Mancur Olson in his doctoral thesis and later book, *The logic of collection action* (1965).

But we do cooperate, and we cooperate more than would be predicted by Olson's thesis (Ostrom, 1998). And expectations derived from an understanding of the role that expressive motivation plays are key here. This is because the process of confirming her values and identity motivates the rational public employee to create a sense of attachment with others who share her values (Schuessler, 2000). This group formation enables individuals who are expressively motivated to engage in collective action. But the focus of this collective action is the *direct* benefits that are generated from the action itself (Jennings, 2015). It is the process of participating in collective action as a means of confirming values and political beliefs that is the focus of such action; whether the collective action results in any instrumental outcomes (including negative and unintended social consequences) is immaterial to such expressively motivated collective action.

It is also the case that action based on such collective group identity may have other negative consequences. In such cases, the rational actors' confirmation of identity often involves reference to a rival group who hold different values (Hamlin and Jennings, 2019). This has potentially serious consequences in the provision of public services if such rival groups are politicians or the public.

Expressive motivation and public service motivation theory

My argument here – that observed public service motivation is not an alternative to, but consistent with, rational choice theory – is arguably consistent with some tenets of PSMT.

First, public service motivation is about individual motivation and how it drives behaviour. There is also recognition within the literature that the connection between motive and action is moderated by the institutional settings within which actors make decisions. This approach is consistent with rational choice at a number of levels.

Second, PSMT recognises that public servants have mixed motivations for their behaviours. Rational choice also posits that public employees will have mixed motives – both a mixture of rational motives (instrumental, expressive, self-regarding and other regarding), and non-rational motives such as emotion. While controversial, PSMT often acknowledges that public service-motivated employees have rational motives that drive their public spiritness.

Finally, several PSMT authors have discussed the relationship between identity and public service motivation. Perry and Vandenabeele (2008), Pedersen (2015), Schott et al (2015) and Wang et al (2020) have all discussed this relationship.

Although there are some similarities between expressive motivation and PSMT, and while some PSMT authors have discussed the relationship between public service motivation and identity, there are important consequential differences that need to be raised.

First, expressively motivated employees are intrinsically motivated to work in the public sector because they enjoy the work they do. Both the expressive account and public service motivation share this view of public actors' motivations. It is entirely consistent with understanding of human motivation rooted in rationalism. Further, the public sector can provide identifiable and relevant conditions (Frey, 1997) under which this intrinsic motivation could be crowded out by monetary incentives (Frey, 1997).

Second, expressively motivated public employees might support a policy position or public service even knowing that the policy or service is ineffective. Expressive utility is derived from being seen to support a policy or service; an important assumption of expressive motivation is that the public employee does not take into account the effect on others or whether the policy or service works. This in part explains the 'we must do something' approach to public service provision, as well as the continuation of public programmes that are known to be ineffective or even harmful.

The third possible consequence might also be seen as a negative. Expressively motivated public employees might engage in behaviours that result in expressive policy traps.

Expressive policy traps

An expressive policy trap occurs when, collectively, public actors propose or support a policy that individually they would oppose because it is harmful to them. It is expressively motivated behaviour taken by a rational individual that would be different to the action that would be taken if they were instrumentally motivated. In a policy making environment, this may mean that individuals use this opportunity to promote or support policy initiatives which positively reflect on their values and identity, but for which they would not instrumentally support. In collective settings such as policy networks or policy-focused team discussions, the cost of expressively promoting a policy intervention is relatively low. It may be some time before the policy is implemented, and even longer before it has any real effect, whereas the expressive benefit of promoting the policy and getting positive feedback from colleagues is a direct and immediate one.

At an individual level, this is low cost, low risk behaviour and generates expressive benefits. But the collective outcome of a group or groups of actors expressively supporting a policy proposal that instrumentally they would not, would create expressive policy traps. Policies get implemented, and public money gets spent, on policies that are not in the individual self-interest of those promoting them. These expressive policy traps can have serious consequences. There are a number of interventions that are promoted, funded and implemented even though there is considerable evidence that the intervention does not generate the outcomes desired. The intervention or programme is nevertheless promoted because of its value-expressive benefits. The danger is that such policies are inefficient, ineffective, or work against public values. The opposite of this is that policy interventions are rejected – even when there is evidence of their effectiveness – because of expressive policy traps.

Ayre Hillman (2010) sets out a number of examples of expressive policy traps, but focuses on traps that arise because of voters' support for policy proposals at elections. There are, however, clear examples of expressive policy traps arising from public actors' actions.

Take, for example, a political party that promotes the abolition of private schools while one or more of its senior politicians send their children to a fee-charging school. The expressive utility gained from collectively promoting this policy stands contrary to the individual instrumental benefit derived from their children's education. What looks like hypocrisy could be a perfectly rational expressive policy trap.

Equally, civil servants might collectively promote a welfare reform policy that leads to higher spending and higher taxation, even where individually the policy means higher tax take from their salary.

A recent possible example of this in the UK has been senior officials publicly and collectively supporting lockdowns and other restrictions during the COVID-19 pandemic, while individually ignoring the restrictions.

This is not to suggest that expressive motivation only leads to negative outcomes. Expressive motivation can and does lead to a number of prosocial benefits. But the issue is that what is driving this behaviour is not the benefit it generates for others, but the benefit it generates for the actor whose prosocial values and identity are confirmed by these behaviours. The expressively motivated actor does not internalise the benefit (or cost) that their behaviour has on others (Hillman, 2010).

Let me further illustrate this with a non-public administration example. Around Manchester and other cities in England, there are posters asking individuals not to give money to people experiencing street homelessness, and a number of homelessness charities have run campaigns to discourage such giving. There are many reasons for this. For example, people experiencing street homelessness are 17 times more likely than the general population to be the victim of a crime (O'Leary, 2004), often crimes including being mugged, or being abused by organised criminals who use them as fronts to generate income. Yet even when this is known, individuals still give money directly to people experiencing street homelessness. This is an example of what is called *expressive generosity*. The act of giving provides expressive utility to the giver, who confirms their charitable and caring values to themselves, but who is indifferent to the negative consequences that might generate for the individual experiencing street homelessness. Expressive generosity has been demonstrated in a number of experiments (Hillman, 2010).

But it is important to stress that a purely expressively motivated actor would be rare. For most of us, our behaviour is driven by a mix of motives, instrumental and expressive. While I have set out that the unique features of public institutions may affect this mix so that public employees are more expressively motivated than those not working in the public sector, they will nevertheless also be instrumentality motivated (and indeed, affected by non-rational motives too).

Often, the actions driven by instrumental and expressive motives will be similar. A public employee might advocate a policy position, or take action with regards to the distribution of public resources, in a way that is consistent with both their instrumental and expressive motives. At other times, rational actors will trade off between these motives.

Here, again, the institutional design of the public organisation, its form and function and the policy area or areas it covers will have an effect on the extent to which expressive motivation affects behaviour and collective decisions. Colin Jennings (2015) has argued that differences in the governance landscape between health and education in England will have an effect on the extent to which individual voters express support for particular policies in elections, and it is reasonable to suspect that such differences will also be significant to policy makers and other public employees. The publicness of the organisation, its geographic and electoral remit, the organisation of the public services and levels of accountability between service providers and political authorities are all institutional design features that are likely to affect action and collective action of expressively motivated public employees.

Testing for expressive motivation in public employees

So far, so good. I have set out an alternative explanation of the motivations of public employees. I have set out some expectations in terms of the behavioural outcomes of this explanation, which are summarised and further developed in Table 6.2.

Table 6.2: Expectations of expressively motivated public employees

Expected outcome	Explanation
Public servants will have a mix of instrumental and expressive motivations.	The mix will depend on a number of factors, both institutional and individual. There may be conflict between behaviour that is instrumental and expressive motivated; there may not be any conflict.
Furthering the public interest is an important value/part of their identity that individuals seek to confirm through public employment.	This value can be both an antecedent and consequence of public sector employment. Individuals for whom this value is important are more likely to seek public sector employment. The public interest norm that is core to much of the public sector will affect and be affected by public employees seeking to confirm this aspect of their identity. Working with others who share these values may gain expressive utility from this group identity, but this may cause conflict with other rival groups which would be avoided though more instrumentally motivated behaviour.
The extent to which *furthering the public interest* is an instrumental or expressive goal will depend on whether there are identifiable beneficiaries, the extent to which the actor understands whether they have made a contribution, and whether the public interest outcome is observable.	Public employees are more likely to be instrumentally motivated to further the public interest where there are clearly defined beneficiaries, where the outcomes generated by their work are directly observable, and where such outcomes are delivered immediately or within short timescales.

Table 6.2: Expectations of expressively motivated public employees (continued)

Expected outcome	Explanation
Public employees who are expressively motivated to further the public interest will be indifferent to public policy or programme outcomes.	Public employees are more likely to be expressively motivated to confirm their public interestedness identity where there are not clearly defined beneficiaries, where they cannot easily determine whether they have made a positive contribution to the welfare of others, or to the outcomes of public policies, programmes, or services. In such circumstances, public employees do not internalise the costs or benefits to others of their actions but rather the benefits to themselves of confirming their identity.
Expressive policy traps will arise when public actors collectively support policy positions that individually they would not.	Collective action provides a low-cost mechanism through which individuals expressively confirm aspects of their identity and values. This might create conflict between instrumental and expressive utiles, and also create negative or positive externalities.
Expressive rhetoric may result in policies and programmes being funded or maintained despite not achieving policy objectives.	Individual public employees may be expressively motivated to support policies or programmes because doing so confirms parts of their identity or values that are important to them. The effectiveness of the policy or programme is not a material consideration in their decision to support or defend.

But theory in of itself does not give sufficient insight. What is needed is empirical testing of this theory.

There is a small but growing research agenda that empirically examines expressive motivation. This is generally limited to expressive voting. It draws on experimental designs, often using adapted dictator games and public goods games. Alan Hamlin and Colin Jennings provide an overview of some of this literature in their contribution to the recently published *Oxford handbook of public choice* (Hamlin and Jennings, 2019). But outside of expressive voting, there is a very limited empirical literature examining expressive motivation, and none in long-term or repeated contexts such as public employment.

There are of course significant challenges with empirically observing the motives of individuals in any given situation. In the PSMT literature, there are three core approaches to identifying motives: (a) using secondary data, infer motivation from self-reported measures; (b) using cross sectional surveys, ask respondents about their motives; and (c) using experimental designs, and infer motives from the behaviours of respondents. And, in the expressive literature, experiments and survey data have been used in a similar fashion.

Given that there are some very different social outcomes expected from PSMT compared to a model of public employee motivation based in expressive rationality, a research agenda that tests whether expressive motivation plays a role in driving the behaviour of public employees is needed. Of course, given the near hegemonic status in public administration of public service motivation as the explanation of public employees' behaviour, and the obvious normative appeal of PSMT, establishing such a research agenda is likely to be challenging.

However, there are three areas where research could be undertaken that might also benefit the PSMT agenda.

First, several authors have discussed the role that identity may play in public service motivation. This is an area of potential synergy between the expressive motivation and the public service motivation research agendas, with opportunity to develop this further, and to examine ways of empirically exploring the role that identity plays in the motivation and behaviour of public employees.

Second, the public interest and public values play very different roles in PSMT and expressive rationality. If public employees are expressively motivated, questions of how they understand the public interest, and how they know whether they have furthered it, are immaterial. But if they are public service-motivated, then these questions are very material. Empirical research around these issues would be illuminating.

Third, there are different policy outcome expectations derived from the two theories. Despite the unique nature of public organisations in relation to public policy, and the role that attraction to public policy plays in PSMT, there is no literature that uses policy analysis to explore the behavioural consequences of public service motivation. Comparative policy analysis, drawing on the expected policy outcomes derived from both public service motivation and expressive motivation, could contribute to our understanding in this area.

Conclusion

What motivates public employees, and how does that motivation affect their individual and collective behaviour? These are core questions in public administration, and are usually (in part) answered by PSMT. In this chapter, I proposed an alternative explanation. I started with the assumption that public employees, like everyone else, have a number of different motives that drive their behaviour. These motives are self-regarding, and other regarding. They are instrumentally rational motives, and they are expressively rational motives.

Expressive motives drive behaviour where the goal of that behaviour is the act itself. This can include job satisfaction and the meaningfulness of work, and it can also involve communicating values and beliefs, affirming identify to others and the actor herself. While no one is purely expressively motivated, there are specific and unique features of public organisations — particularly the public interest norm — that incentivise greater expressive behaviour. And this has important implications for public policy, and the provision of public services.

In this chapter, I have explored expressive motivation theory and applied it to the motivations of public employees. I have discussed the implications of this, both in terms of the public interest, and in terms of individual and collective decision-making. I have established that the institutional design of public organisations – their publicness, their form and function, the closeness of their services to specific beneficiaries – will be important incentives and constraints that affect the causal pathway between motivation and behaviour.

There are significant implications for the public interest if – as I argue – public employees are expressively motivated. These include the potential for expressive policy traps, where ineffective policies are collectively and expressively supported, even though these same policies would not be supported instrumentally. But so far, I have only theorised that public servants are expressively motivated. This needs to be explored empirically, before any conclusions are drawn that affect real-world public administration.

SEVEN

Conclusion

Critique of public service motivation theory

PSMT is the dominant, if not hegemonic, explanation of the motives and actions of public employees in public administration scholarship. For 30 years, the proposition that public servants answer 'the call to public service', which is seen to be a higher order, other regarding motivation, has reasserted itself in the public administration and public management literature. A wide, impressive and highly impactful empirical literature has demonstrated that public servants are public service-motivated, and has considered the antecedents and consequences of this.

But there are serious issues with this proposition. It is still not clear what public service motivation is, what it is not and how it is different from other concepts of prosocial motives and behaviours. Despite assertions that public service motivation is found in all humans regardless of setting, research on this motivation is still overwhelmingly located in public administration scholarship, and overwhelmingly focused on public employees. Indeed, because of this, this book has focused on public employees and on whether and how PSMT explains their motives and behaviours.

Despite its clear location in furthering the public interest, PSMT fails to explain what the public interest is, how public employees understand the public interest and how they know whether they are in fact furthering it. The public interest is, of course, an abstract, distal and contested concept, which eluded conceptual clarity long before PSMT existed. It is an ideal; and a subjectively conceived and largely contested ideal at that. But given the implicit assertion of the PSMT literature that we should simply trust that public servants are furthering the public interest, there really ought to be a better explanation of how this normative motive directs the behaviour of public servants.

This leads to the second significant gap. The consequences of public service motivation – or indeed any other form of motive, preference, or goal – is behaviour. The link between motive and behaviour is tempered by the incentives and constraints we face in any given social situation. These include the public interest norm, the institutional design features of public organisations – their publicness, their form and function, their closeness to specific beneficiaries – and their organisational mission and values. And the behaviour of public servants has significant implications for citizens, businesses, communities, taxpayers and the like. For public servants make decisions – individual and collective – that have real-world consequences. Questions of how and in what ways the behaviour and decisions of public servants are affected by the motives of public servants, and the consequences of this, should be at the heart of public administration scholarship. But PSMT lacks any consideration of decision-making by public employees.

The final significant issue with PSMT is its empirical evidence. Overwhelmingly, this is drawn from cross-sectional surveys in which the dependent and independent variables are based on self-reported measures. It should be of little surprise that, when asked, public servants do indeed state that they work to further the public interest. The public interest is the dominant language of government, of politicians, public servants, public policy, the judiciary, lobbyists and special interest groups. It is a powerful norm that incentivises and reinforces values, motives and behaviour. In the few instances when PSMT draws on experimental evidence, public service motivation is inferred from examples of prosocial behaviour.

That public employees are motivated by 'the call' and put others before self is normatively very appealing and powerful. But there are two implicit assertions that flow from this that should be challenged.

The first is the notion that government is benign, omnipotent and omniscient. That we should simply trust that public servants know what they are doing, and that they are furthering the public good. But governments make mistakes. Government failure may be as likely as market failure. Policies can fail. They fail for different reasons, and in a variety of ways. They may sometimes work and subsequent fail. They may fail from implementation. There may be general agreement that they have failed, or failure might be contested. They might completely fail, partly fail, or work but generate unintended and negative consequences. Those in government – politicians and public servants – face the same information problems that all of us face. These include: (a) our cognitive limits; (b) the contested, conflicting, contradictory, and incomplete nature of information we use in decision-making; and (c) fundamental uncertainty (that is, we make decisions today about future consequences. The decisions we make are based on the information available to us at the point we make the decision. Yet in many circumstances, information does not exist at the time of our decisions which, when it does become available, makes a material difference to the decision we have made).

The second is that public service motivation is overwhelmingly a positive feature of public servants, and that public organisations should employ more people with higher levels of public service motivation, and should act in ways that increase levels of public service motivation in their workforces. The issue with this is that some of the values that PSMT asserts as core public values are highly politicised and left-leaning.

Public service motivated?

The dominance of PSMT in the public administration literature is such that we are in danger of seeing only one explanation of what motivates public employees. But as many in the field acknowledge, public employees are motivated by a range of factors, of which furthering the public interest is only one. And given the empirical literature to date, there are for me questions of whether what is being observed is in fact consistent with the theory of public service motivation.

In this book, I have set out an alternative explanation of the motives of public employees.

This alternative explanation is rooted in rationality. But I do not assert that rationality is only egotistical and selfish. Rather, rationality is reasoned and goal-orientated behaviour. It is motivated by self-regarding and other regarding goals. It can be instrumental, and it can be expressive.

My thesis is that expressive motivation provides a more complete explanation of the self-reported public interestedness of public employees than does PSMT. This expressive motivation has two elements. First, expressive motivation is intrinsic motivation. Individuals are often motivated to work in the public sector because they enjoy the work that they do. In line with PSMT, I posit that intrinsic motivation is an important energiser of behaviour by public sector employees. However, unlike PSMT, I argue that this intrinsic motivation is entirely consistent with rational choice theory.

The second element of the expressive motivation of public employees relates to their values and identity. My argument here is that the public interest is an important value for public employees and, as such, individuals for whom this value is an important part of their identity will seek out and maintain employment in the public sector. They do so because all individuals are motivated to confirm to self and to others important aspects of identity and values. A rational actor might be motivated to express her values and beliefs, and take action that enables her to do so. She might be motivated by the desire to demonstrate her positive, prosocial attributes of being generous, cooperative, trusting, and her moral values. In doing so, the rational actor might be motivated by self-approval, but also the approval of others.

Core to my argument here – and in common with PSMT – is that furthering the public interest is an important value for public employees.

But the public interest plays a very different role in an expressive account of the motivations of public employees than it does in PSMT. In the expressive account, what is important is not whether an individual public employee makes a contribution to, or has an impact on, the common good. Indeed, this expressively rational actor is indifferent to whether the public interest is actually furthered. Rather, what motivates this expressively rational actor is confirming – both to themselves and by others – this important aspect of their identity.

While expressive rationality has been demonstrated in a range of non-market political behaviours, it has not previously been applied systematically to an explanation of the motives and behaviours of public servants. In this book, I have made such an application. I have set out how the unique nature of public organisations might incentivise public servants to engage in higher levels of expressive behaviour than their private sector counterparts. And while in many cases this might result in the same public outcomes that would arise from public service-motivated or instrumentally other regarding-motivated public servants, there are also potential negative consequences of expressively motivated behaviour. The most significant of these is expressive policy traps, which can result in ineffective and unwanted policy programmes being implemented or continued.

But theory is not enough. While expressive rationality has been empirically evidenced in a number of different settings and contexts, it has not been the field of public administration. Having established theoretically that expressive motivation might explain the behaviour of public servants, empirical research is now needed. I hope that this research will contribute to our knowledge of what motivates the behaviour of public servants.

Appendix

A search was conducted in January 2020 on Web of Science for articles with the term 'Public Service Motivation' in the article title. A total of n=52 articles were retrieved. Descriptive data were extracted by the author from all n=52 articles: including whether the article was empirical or theoretical in nature; the type of method used; the population sampled in the research; and the focus of the empirical research (whether PSM was considered in the underlying research as an antecedent, consequence, or moderator, and the key research question being considered). The appendix table provides a summary of the extracted descriptive data.

Articles published in 2020 containing 'public service motivation' in title

Authors	Empirical	Population	Country	Research method				Focus			Moderator	Area of interest
				Quants	Secondary data	Quals		Antecedents	Consequences			
Alcoba and Phinaitrup	Yes	Social workers	Philippines	Yes							Yes	
Asseburg and Homberg	Yes	Students	Germany	Yes						Yes		Sector attraction
Belrhiti, Van Damme and Belalia	Yes	Health workers	Morocco			Yes		Yes				How to increase PSM
Boyd and Newell	Yes	University staff	US	Yes						Yes		Employee wellbeing and engagement
Bright	Yes	Federal employees	US	Yes						Yes		Job satisfaction
Bromberg and Charbonneau	Yes	HR employees	US and international	Yes						Yes		Personality and PSM and recruitment
Caillier	Yes	General population	US	Yes						Yes		Leadership

(continued)

Authors	Empirical	Population	Country	Research method				Focus			Moderator	Area of interest
				Quants	Secondary data	Quals		Antecedents	Consequences			
Cheng, Chang and Lee	Yes	Utility sector workers	Taiwan	Yes					Yes			Organisational Citizenship Behaviour
Corduneanu, Dudau and Kominis	No											Self-determination theory and PSM
Davis, Stazyk and Klingeman	Yes	Federal employees	US	Yes	Yes				Yes			Whistle-blowing
Fennimore	Yes	General population	US	Yes					Yes			Communal narcissists
Gans-Morse, Kalgin, Klimenko and Vorobyev	Yes	Students	Russia	Yes					Yes			Sector attraction
Gan, Ling and Wang	Yes	Public employees undertaking MPA	China	Yes					Yes			Performance

(continued)

145

Authors	Empirical	Population	Country	Research method				Focus			Area of interest
				Quants	Secondary data	Quals	Antecedents	Consequences	Moderator		
Gupta, Dash, Kakka and Yadav	Yes	Federal employees	India	Yes				Yes		Job satisfaction
Hassan, Zhang, Ahmad, and Liu	Yes	University staff	Iraq	Yes				Yes		Organisational change
Hostrup and Andersen	Yes	Police and counselling	Denmark	Yes		Yes		Yes		Leadership
Ingrams	Yes	Public employees	US	Yes	Yes			Yes		Organisational Citizenship Behaviour
Kalgin	No									Literature review of Russian studies
Kerrissey, Wilkerson and Meyers	Yes	General population	US	Yes	Yes			Yes		Political participation
Ki	Yes	General population	Florida, US	Yes	Yes			Yes		Willingness to learn

(continued)

Authors	Empirical	Population	Country	Research method				Focus			Moderator	Area of interest
				Quants	Secondary data	Quals		Antecedents	Consequences			
Kim	Yes	Students	Korea	Yes	Yes			Yes				Level of education
Tuan	Yes	Local authority employees	Vietnam	Yes					Yes		Yes	Humility and job crafting
Meyer-Sahling, Mikkelsen and Schuster	Yes	Public employees	International	Yes				Yes				How to increase PSM
Mikkelsen, Schuster and Meyer-Sahling	Yes	Public employees	International	Yes								Measurement tool validation
Mussagulova	Yes	Public employees	Moldova	Yes					Yes			Work engagement
Papenfuß and Keppeler	No											Narrative review of literature on PSM and performance-relatedpay

(continued)

Authors	Empirical	Population	Country	Research method			Focus			Moderator	Area of interest
				Quants	Secondary data	Quals	Antecedents	Consequences			
Pautz and Vogel	Yes	University staff	US?	Yes				Yes			Faculty motivation
Peretz	Yes	Public security and public health	Israel			Yes		Yes			Work engagement
Perry	No										Editorial comment
Piatak and Holt (a)	Yes	General population	US	Yes	Yes			Yes			Organisational Citizenship Behaviour
Piatak and Holt (b)	Yes	General population	US	Yes	Yes			Yes			Prosocial behaviours
Piatak, Sowa, Jacobson and Johnson	No										HR implications of PSM
Potipiroon and Wongpreedee	Yes	Local authority employees	Thailand	Yes				Yes	Yes		Whistle-blowing

(continued)

Authors	Empirical	Population	Country	Research method			Focus			Moderator	Area of interest
				Quants	Secondary data	Quals	Antecedents	Consequences			
Potipiroon and Faerman	Yes	Local authority employees	Thailand	Yes				Yes		Yes	Occupational Citizenship Behaviour
Prysmakova and Vandenabeele	Yes	Police	Poland and Belgium	Yes				Yes			Job satisfaction
Prysmakova	Yes	Local authority employees	US?	Yes				Yes			Job satisfaction
Ripoll and Schott	Yes	General population	Catalonia, Spain	Yes				Yes			Unethical behaviour
Ritz, Schott, Nitzl and Alfes	Yes	Public employees	Bern, Switzerland	Yes	Yes			Yes			Political participation
Scheller and Reglen	Yes	Fire fighters	Texas, US	Yes				Yes			Performance
Schwartz, Eva and Newman	Yes	Public employees	China	Yes			Yes	Yes			Leadership and performance

(continued)

Authors	Empirical	Population	Country	Research method				Focus		Moderator	Area of interest
				Quants	Secondary data	Quals		Antecedents	Consequences		
Sukhumvito, Yuniawan, Kusumawardhani, Udin	Yes	Public employees	Indonesia	Yes					Yes		Performance
Slabbinck and Van Witteloostuijn	Yes	Students	Belgium and Netherlands	Yes				Yes			Basic human motives
Stefurak, Morgan and Johnson	Yes	Emergency medical personnel	US	Yes					Yes		Performance and job satisfaction
Sukowski, Przytula, Borg and Kulikowski	Yes	University staff	Poland and Malta			Yes			Yes		Performance
Tuan, Rowley, Khai, Qian, Masli and Le	Yes	Local authority employees	Vietnam	Yes					Yes	Yes	Performance and job satisfaction
Vandenabeele and Jager	Yes	Students	Netherlands	Yes					Yes	Yes	Recruitment

(continued)

Authors	Empirical	Population	Country	Research method			Focus			Area of interest
				Quants	Secondary data	Quals	Antecedents	Consequences	Moderator	
Vogel	Yes	Public employees	Omaha, US			Yes				Relationship between calling and PSM
Wang and Seifert	Yes	Local authority employees	England	Yes				Yes		BAME employees, fairness, PSM
Wang, van Witteloostuijn and Heine	No									Morality and PSM
Ward and Miller-Stevens	Yes	Not-for-profit board members	US	Yes				Yes		Sector of employment and PSM and effect on volunteering
Weißmüller, De Waele and van Witteloostuijn	Yes	Students	Belgium, Germany and Netherlands	Yes				Yes		Prosocial rule-breaking
Zhang, Wu and Graham	Yes	Police staff	UK	Yes				Yes		Job satisfaction

References

Abner, G.B., Kim, S.Y. and Perry, J.L. (2017) 'Building evidence for public human resource management: using middle range theory to link theory and data.' *Review of Public Personnel Administration*, 37(2): 139–59.

Akerlof, G. and Kranton, R. (2010) *Identity economics: how our identities shape our work, wages, and wellbeing.* Oxford: Princeton University Press.

Alcoba, R.C. and Phinaitrup, B.A. (2020) 'In search of the Holy Grail in public service: a study on the mediating effect of public service motivation on organizational politics and outcomes.' *International Journal of Public Administration*, 43(1): 73–83.

Anderfuhren-Biget, S., Varone, F. and Giauque, D. (2014) 'Policy environment and public service motivation.' *Public Administration*, 92(4): 807–25.

Andersen, L.B. and Serritzlew, S. (2012) 'Does public service motivation affect the behavior of professionals?' *International Journal of Public Administration*, 35(1): 19–29.

Andersen, L.B., Jorgensen, T.B., Kjeldsen, A.M., Pedersen, L.H. and Vrangbaek, K. (2013) 'Public values and public service motivation: conceptual and empirical relationships.' *American Review of Public Administration*, 43(3): 292–311.

Andreoni, J. (1990) 'Impure altruism and donations to public-goods: a theory of warm-glow giving.' *Economic Journal*, 100(401): 464–77.

Awan, S., Esteve, M. and van Witteloostuijn, A. (2020) 'Talking the talk, but not walking the walk: Aa comparison of self-reported and observed prosocial behaviour.' *Public Administration*, 98(4): 995–1010.

Belle, N. and Ongaro, E. (2014) 'NPM, administrative reforms and public service motivation: improving the dialogue between research agendas.' *International Review of Administrative Sciences*, 80(2): 382–400.

Bhatti, Y., Olsen, A.L. and Pedersen, L.H. (2009) 'The effects of administrative professionals on contracting out.' *Governance: An International Journal of Policy Administration and Institutions*, 22(1): 121–37.

Blais, A. and Dion, S. (1990) 'Are bureaucrats budget maximizers? The Niskanen model and its critics.' *Polity*, 22(4): 655–74.

Bolino, M.C. and Grant, A.M. (2016) 'The bright side of being prosocial at work, and the dark side, too: a review and agenda for research on other-oriented motives, behavior, and impact in organizations.' *Academy of Management Annals*, 10(1): 599–670.

Boruvka, E. and Perry, J.L. (2020) 'Understanding evolving public motivational practices: an institutional analysis.' *Governance: An International Journal of Policy Administration and Institutions*, 33(3): 565–84.

Bozeman, B. (2007) *Public values and public interest: counterbalancing economic individualism.* Washington, DC: Georgetown University Press.

Bozeman, B. and Su, X.H. (2015) 'Public service motivation concepts and theory: a critique.' *Public Administration Review*, 75(5): 700–10.

Brewer, G.A. (2008) 'Employee and organizational performance.' In J. Perry and A. Hondeghem (eds) *Motivation in public management: the call of public service.* Oxford: Oxford University Press.

Brewer, G.A. (2019) 'Public service motivation: overcoming major obstacles to research progress.' In A. Massey (ed) *A research agenda for public administration.* Cheltenham: Edward Elgar.

Brewer, G.A., Selden, S.C. and Facer, R.L. (2000) 'Individual conceptions of public service motivation.' *Public Administration Review*, 60(3): 254–64.

Bright, L. (2008) 'Does public service motivation really make a difference on the job satisfaction and turnover intentions of public employees?' *American Review of Public Administration*, 38(2): 149–66.

Bromberg, D.E. and Charbonneau, E. (2020) 'Public service motivation, personality, and the hiring decisions of public managers: an experimental study.' *Public Personnel Management*, 49(2): 193–217.

Brunnschweiler, C.N., Jennings, C. and MacKenzie, I.A. (2014) 'A study of expressive choice and strikes.' *European Journal of Political Economy*, 49(2): 111–25.

Caillier, J.G. (2014) 'Toward a better understanding of the relationship between transformational leadership, public service motivation, mission valence, and employee performance: a preliminary study.' *Public Personnel Management*, 43(2): 218–39.

Caillier, J.G. (2017) 'Public service motivation and decisions to report wrongdoing in US federal agencies: is this relationship mediated by the seriousness of the wrongdoing.' *American Review of Public Administration*, 47(7): 810–25.

Caplan, B. (2001) 'Rational irrationality and the microfoundations of political failure.' *Public Choice*, 107(3–4): 311–31.

Chen, C.A., Hsieh, C.W. and Chen, D.Y. (2014) 'Fostering public service motivation through workplace trust: evidence from public managers in Taiwan.' *Public Administration*, 92(4): 954–73.

Cheng, K.T., Chang, Y.C. and Lee, C. (2020) 'The effect of public service motivation at individual, group, and organisational levels of citizenship behaviour.' *Information Resources Management Journal*, 33(1): 39–58.

Chong, D. (2000) *Rational lives: norms and values in politics and society*. Chicago, IL: Chicago University Press.

Christensen, J. (2011) 'Competing theories of regulatory governance: reconsidering public interest theory of regulation.' In D. Levi-Faur (ed) *Handbook on the politics of regulation*. Cheltenham: Edward Elgar.

Christensen, R.K. and Wright, B.E. (2011) 'The effects of public service motivation on job choice decisions: disentangling the contributions of person-organization fit and person-job fit.' *Journal of Public Administration Research and Theory*, 21(4): 723–43.

Cochran, C.E. (1974) 'Political science and "the public interest."' *Journal of Politics*, 36(2): 327–55.

Cooper, C.A. (2020) 'Public servants, anonymity, and political activity online: bureaucratic neutrality in peril.' *International Review of Administrative Sciences*, 86(3): 496–512.

Cooper, C.A. and Reinagel, T.P. (2017) 'The limits of public service motivation: confidence in government institutions among public servants.' *Administration & Society*, 49(9): 1297–317.

Cooper, D., Lowe, A., Puxty, A., Robson, K. and Willmott, H. (1988) 'Regulating the UK accountancy profession: episodes in the relation between the profession and the state.' In ESRC Conference on Corporatism. London: Policy Studies Institute.

Cope, S. (2000) 'Assessing rational choice models of budgeting: from budget maximising to bureau shaping: a case study of British local government.' *Journal of Public Budgeting, Accounting and Financial Management*, 12(4): 598–624.

Corduneanu, R., Dudau, A. and Kominis, G. (2020) 'Crowding-in or crowding-out: the contribution of self-determination theory to public service motivation.' *Public Management Review*, 22(7): 1070–89.

Coursey, D.H., Perry, J.L., Brudney, J.L. and Littlepage, L. (2008) 'Psychometric verification of Perry's public service motivation instrument results for volunteer exemplars.' *Review of Public Personnel Administration*, 28(1): 79–90.

Crewson, P.E. (1997) 'Public-service motivation: building empirical evidence of incidence and effect.' *Journal of Public Administration Research and Theory*, 7(4): 499–518.

Cribb, J., Davenport, A. and Zaranko, B. (2019) 'Public sector pay and employment. Where are we now?' IFS Briefing Note BN263. London: Institute for Fiscal Studies.

Croley, S.P. (2008) *Regulation and public interests: the possibility of good regulatory government.* Oxford: Princeton University Press.

Cruess, S.R., Johnston, S. and Cruess, R.L. (2004) ' "Profession": a working definition for medical educators.' *Teaching and Learning in Medicine*, 16(1): 74–6.

Davis, R.S., Stazyk, E.C. and Klingeman, C.M. (2020) 'Accounting for personal disposition and organizational context: connecting role ambiguity, public service motivation, and whistle-blowing in federal agencies.' *International Journal of Human Resource Management*, 31(10): 1313–32.

Dawson, C., Baker, P.L. and Dowell, D. (2019) 'Getting into the "giving habit": the dynamics of volunteering in the UK.' *Voluntas*, 30(5): 1006–21.

Deci, E. and Ryan, R. (1985) *Intrinsic motivation and self-determination in human behavior*. New York, NY: Plenum.

Dollery, B. and Hamburger, P. (1996) 'Modelling bureaucracy: the case of the Australian federal budget sector 1982–1992.' *Public Administration*, 74(3): 477–507.

Dow, S.C. (2015) 'Addressing uncertainty in economics and the economy.' *Cambridge Journal of Economics*, 39(1): 33–47.

Dowding, K. and James, O. (2004) 'Analysing bureau-shaping models: comments on Marsh, Smith and Richards.' *British Journal of Political Science*, 34(1): 183–92.

Downs, A. (1967) *Inside bureaucracy*. Ann Arbor, MI: University of Michigan.

Downs, A. (1997 [1957]) *Economic theory of democracy*. London: Pearson.

Dunleavy, P. (1991) *Democracy, bureaucracy and public choice: economic explanations in political science*. Harlow: Prentice Hall.

Dunleavy, P. and Hood, C. (1994) 'From old public-administration to new public management.' *Public Money & Management*, 14(3): 9–16.

Dunleavy, P., Margetts, H., Bastow, S. and Tinkler, J. (2006) 'New public management is dead: long live digital-era governance.' *Journal of Public Administration Research and Theory*, 16(3): 467–94.

Elster, J. (2006) 'Altruistic behaviour and altruistic motivations.' In S. Kolm and J. Ytheir (eds) *Handbook on the economics of giving, reciprocity, and altruism*. London: Elsevier.

Elster, J. (2009) 'Emotional choice and rational choice.' In P. Goldie (ed) *The Oxford handbook of philosophy of emotion*. Oxford: Oxford University Press.

Ertas, N. (2020) 'How public, nonprofit, and private-sector employees access volunteer roles.' *Journal of Nonprofit & Public Sector Marketing*, 32(2): 105–23.

Fan, Y.M. (2015) 'The centre decides and the local pays: mandates and politics in local government financial management in China.' *Local Government Studies*, 41(4): 516–33.

Fedele, A. and Giannoccolo, P. (2020) 'Paying politicians: not too little, not too much.' *Economica*, 87(346): 470–89.

Fennimore, A.K. (2021) 'Duplicitous me: communal narcissists and public service motivation.' *Public Personnel Management*, 50(1): 25–55.

Ferlie, E. (2017) *The new public management and public management studies. Oxford research encyclopedia of business and management*. Oxford: Oxford University Press.

Finkelstein, M. (2011) 'Intrinsic and extrinsic motivation and organizational citizenship behavior: a functional approach to organizational citizenship behavior.' *Journal of Psychological Issues in Organizational Culture*, 2(1): 19–34.

Freidson, E. (1970) *Profession of medicine: a study of the sociology of applied knowledge*. New York, NY: Dodd Mead.

Freidson, E. (1986) *Professional powers: a study of the institutionalisation of formal knowledge*. Chicago, IL: University of Chicago Press.

Frey, B. (1997) *Not just for the money: an economic theory of personal motivation*. Cheltenham: Edward Elgar.

Gailmard, S. (2010) 'Politics, principal-agent problems, and public service motivation.' *International Public Management Journal*, 13(1): 35–45.

Gains, F. and John, P. (2010) 'What do bureaucrats like doing? Bureaucratic preferences in response to institutional reform.' *Public Administration Review*, 70(3): 455–63.

Gans-Morse, J., Kalgin, A., Klimenko, A., Vorobyev, D. and Yakovlev, A. (2020) 'Public service motivation and sectoral employment in Russia: new perspectives on the attraction vs. socialization debate.' *International Public Management Journal*. DOI: 10.1080/10967494.2020.1841692

Giauque, D., Ritz, A., Varone, F. and Anderfuhren-Biget, S. (2012) 'Resigned but satisfied: the negative impact of public service motivation and red tape on work satisfaction.' *Public Administration*, 90(1): 175–93.

Grant, A.M. (2008) 'Does intrinsic motivation fuel the prosocial fire? Motivational synergy in predicting persistence, performance, and productivity.' *Journal of Applied Psychology*, 93(1): 48–58.

Grant, A.M. and Berg, J. (2010) 'Prosocial motivation at work: how making a difference makes a difference.' In K. Cameron and G. Spreitzer (eds) *Handbook of positive organizational scholarship*. Oxford: Oxford University Press.

Green, D. and Shapiro, I. (1995) *Pathologies in rational choice: a critique of applications in political science*. New Haven, CT: Yale University Press.

Greenwood, E. (1957) 'Attributes of a profession.' *Social Work*, 2(3): A45–55.

Hamlin, A. and Jennings, C. (2011) 'Expressive political behaviour: foundations, scope and implications.' *British Journal of Political Science*, 41(3): 645–70.

Hamlin, A. and Jennings, C. (2019) 'Expressive voting.' In R. Congleton, B. Grofman and S. Voigt (eds) The Oxford handbook of public choice. New York, NY: Oxford University Press.

Hantke-Domas, M. (2003) 'The public interest theory of regulation: non-existence or misinterpretation?' *European Journal of Law and Economics*, 15(2): 165–95.

Hartley, J., Alford, J., Knies, E. and Douglas, S. (2017) 'Towards an empirical research agenda for public value theory.' *Public Management Review*, 19(5): 670–85.

Hechter, M. and Kanazawa, S. (1997) 'Sociological rational choice theory.' *Annual Review of Sociology*, 23(1): 191–214.

Held, V. (1970) *Public interests and private interests*. New York, NY: Basic Books.

Herne, K. and Setala, M. (2004) 'A response to the critique of rational choice theory: Lakatos' and Laudan's conceptions applied.' *Inquiry: an Interdisciplinary Journal of Philosophy*, 47(1): 67–85.

Hillman, A.L. (2010) 'Expressive behavior in economics and politics.' *European Journal of Political Economy*, 26(4): 403–18.

Hindmoor, A. (2006) *Rational choice*. Basingstoke: Palgrave Macmillan.

Hodgson, G. (2012) 'On the limits of rational choice theory.' *Economic Thought*, 1(1): 94–108.

Hood, C. (1991) 'A public management for all seasons.' *Public Administration*, 69(1): 3–19.

Horton, S. (2008) 'History and persistence of an idea and ideal.' In J. Perry and A. Hondeghem (eds) *Motivation in public management: the call of public service*. New York, NY: Oxford University Press.

Houston, D. (2000) 'Public service motivation: a multivariate test.' *Journal of Public Administration Research and Theory*, 10(4): 713–28.

Houston, D. (2008) 'Behavior in the public square.' In J. Perry and A. Hondeghem (eds) *Motivation in public management: the call to public service*. Oxford: Oxford University Press.

Houston, D., Harding, L. and Whaley, L. (2007) 'Understanding public attitudes about government administrators: perceptions of administrators as public stewards.' Chicago, IL: Mid-West Political Science Association annual conference.

Iannaccone, L.R. (1992) 'Religious markets and the economics of religion.' *Social Compass*, 39(1): 123–31.

Ingrams, A. (2020) 'Organizational citizenship behavior in the public and private sectors: a multilevel test of public service motivation and traditional antecedents.' *Review of Public Personnel Administration*, 40(2): 222–44.

James, O. (2003) *The executive agency revolution in Whitehall: public interest versus bureau-shaping perspectives*. London: Palgrave Macmillan.

Jankowski, R. (2015) *Altruism and self-interest in democracies*. New York: Palgrave Macmillan.

Jennings, C. (2015) 'Collective choice and individual action: education policy and social mobility in England.' *European Journal of Political Economy*, 40(Part B): 288–97.

Jensen, U.T. and Andersen, L.B. (2015) 'Public service motivation, user orientation, and prescription behaviour: doing good for society or for the individual user?' *Public Administration*, 93(3): 753–68.

Jensen, U.T., Andersen, L.B. and Holten, A.L. (2019) 'Explaining a dark side: public service motivation, presenteeism, and absenteeism.' *Review of Public Personnel Administration*, 39(4): 487–510.

Jensen, U.T., Kjeldsen, A. and Vestergaard, C. (2020) 'How is public service motivation affected by regulatory policy changes?' *International Public Management Journal*, 23(4): 465–95.

Jordan, S. (2007) 'The public interest in public administration: an investigation of the communicative foundations of the public interest standard.' PhD. Texas A&M University. [Accessed on 5 January 2021] https://core.ac.uk/download/pdf/4272876.pdf

Jorgensen, T.B. and Bozeman, B. (2007) 'Public values: an inventory.' *Administration & Society*, 39(3): 354–81.

Kerrissey, J., Wilkerson, T. and Meyers, N. (2020) 'The political and civic lives of public sector workers: unions and "public service motivation".' *Sociological Forum*, 19 Nov.

Ki, N. (2020) 'Public service motivation and government officials' willingness to learn in public sector benchmarking process.' *Public Management Review*, 23(4): 610–32.

Kim, S. (2006) 'Public service motivation and organizational citizenship behavior in Korea.' *International Journal of Manpower*, 27(7–8): 722–40.

Kim, S. (2009) 'Revising Perry's measurement scale of public service motivation.' *American Review of Public Administration*, 39(2): 149–63.

Kim, S. (2013) 'Investigating the structure and meaning of public service motivation across populations: developing an international instrument and addressing issues of measurement invariance.' *Journal of Public Administration Research and Theory*, 23(1): 79–102.

Kim, S. (2016) 'Job characteristics, public service motivation, and work performance in Korea.' *Gestion et Management Public*, 5(1): 7–24.

Kim, S. (2020) 'Education and public service motivation: a longitudinal study of high school graduates.' *Public Administration Review*, 81(2): 260–72.

Kim, S. and Vandenabeele, W. (2010) 'A strategy for building public service motivation research internationally.' *Public Administration Review*, 70(5): 701–09.

Kim, S., Vandenabeele, W., Wright, B.E., Andersen, L.B., Cerase, F.P., Christensen, R.K., Desmarais, C., Koumenta, M. et al (2013) 'Investigating the structure and meaning of public service motivation across populations: developing an international instrument and addressing issues of measurement invariance.' *Journal of Public Administration Research and Theory*, 23(1): 79–102.

Kim, S.H. and Kim, S. (2016a) 'National culture and social desirability bias in measuring public service motivation.' *Administration & Society*, 48(4): 444–76.

Kim, S.H. and Kim, S. (2016b) 'Social desirability bias in measuring public service motivation.' *International Public Management Journal*, 19(3): 293–319.

Kleiner, M. and Krueger, A. (2008) 'The prevalence and effects of occupational licensing'. NBER Working Paper 14308, Cambridge, MA: NBER.

Knoke, D. and Wright-Isak, C. (1982) 'Individual motives and organisational incentive systems.' *Research in the sociology of organisations*, 1(2): 209–54.

Koehler, M. and Rainey, H. (2008) 'Interdisciplinary foundations of public service motivation.' In J.L. Perry and A. Hondeghem (eds) *Motivation in public management: the call of public service.* Oxford: Oxford University Press.

Kuo, N.L. (2012) 'Citizen dissatisfaction leads to budget cuts, or not: a case study of a local Taiwanese government.' *Australian Journal of Public Administration*, 71(2): 159–66.

Lasswell, H. (1936) *Politics: who gets what, how, when.* New York: Whittlesey House.

Le Grand, J. (2003) *Motivation, agency, and public policy: of knights and knaves, pawns and queens.* Oxford: Oxford University Press.

Le Grand, J. (2010) 'Knights and knaves return: public service motivation and the delivery of public services.' *International Public Management Journal*, 13(1): 56–71.

Lee, H., Oh, H. and Park, S. (2020) 'Do trust and culture matter for public service motivation development? Evidence from public sector employees in Korea.' *Public Personnel Management*, 49(2): 290–323.

Leisink, P. and Steijn, B. (2008) 'Recruitment, attraction, and selection.' In J.L. Perry and A. Hondeghem (eds) *Motivation in public management: the call of public service*. Oxford: Oxford University Press.

Lipsky, M. (1980) *Street-level bureaucracy: dilemmas of the individual in public services*. New York, NY: Russell Sage Foundation.

Liu, B.C., Tang, N.Y. and Zhu, X.M. (2008) 'Public service motivation and job satisfaction in China: an investigation of generalisability and instrumentality.' *International Journal of Manpower*, 29(8): 684–99.

Liu, T.T., Liu, C.E. and Zhou, E.H. (2019) 'Influence of organizational citizenship behavior on prosocial rule breaking: moral licensing perspective.' *Social Behavior and Personality*, 47(6): 1–9.

Locke, E.A. and Latham, G.P. (1990) 'Work motivation and satisfaction: light at the end of the tunnel.' *Psychological Science*, 1(4): 240–6.

MacDonald, K. (1995) *The sociology of the professions*. London: Sage.

Maesschalck, J., van der Wal, Z. and Huberts, L. (2008) 'Public service motivation and ethical conduct.' In J. Perry and A. Hondeghem (eds) *Motivation in public management: the call of public service*. Oxford: Oxford University Press.

Matthewson, D.J. (1996) 'Welfare reform and comparative models of bureaucratic behavior: budget maximizers and bureau shapers in the United States and France.' *American Review of Public Administration*, 26(2): 135–58.

McCarthy, D., Wei, P., Homberg, F. and Tamvuma, V. (2021) 'Public service motivation in the Chinese public and private sectors.' *Evidence-based HRM: a Global Forum for Empirical Scholarship*, 9(1): 1–17.

Meier, S. (2006) A survey of economic theories and field evidence on pro-social behavior. FRB of Boston Working Paper No. 06-6. http://dx.doi.org/10.2139/ssrn.917187

Meyer, R.E., Egger-Peitler, I., Hollerer, M.A. and Hammerschmid, G. (2014) 'Of bureaucrats and passionate public managers: institutional logics, executive identities, and public service motivation.' *Public Administration*, 92(4): 861–85.

Meynhardt, T. and Jasinenko, A. (2020) 'Measuring public value: scale development and construct validation.' *International Public Management Journal*, 24(2): 222–49.

Modarresi, S., Newman, D.L. and Abolafia, M.Y. (2001) 'Academic evaluators versus practitioners: alternative experiences of professionalism.' *Evaluation and Program Planning*, 24(1): 1–11.

Neumann, O. (2019) ' "Giving something back to society": a study exploring the role of reciprocity norms in public service motivation.' *Review of Public Personnel Administration*, 39(2): 159–84.

Niskanen, W. (1971) *Bureaucracy and representative government.* New York: Transaction Publishers.

Niskanen, W. (2001) 'Bureaucracy.' In W. Shughart and L. Razzolini (eds) *The Elgar Companion to Public Choice.* Cheltenham: Edward Elgar.

Noordegraaf, M. and van Bockel, J. (2006) 'Identifying identities: performance-driven, but professional public managers.' *International Journal of Public Sector Management*, 19(8): 585–97.

O'Leary, C. (2004) *Supporting people benefits realisation.* London: Office of the Deputy Prime Minister.

O'Leary, C. (2015) 'Who benefits? Comparing public and private interest explanations of professions regulation public policy.' PhD Public Policy. London: King's College.

O'Leary, C. (2019) 'Public service motivation: a rationalist critique.' *Public Personnel Management*, 48(1): 82–96.

Olson, M. (1965) *The logic of collective action.* Cambridge, MA: Harvard University Press.

Opp, K. D. (1999) 'Contending conceptions of the theory of rational action.' *Journal of Theoretical Politics*, 11(2): 171–202.

Organ, D. (1988) *The good soldier syndrome*. Lexington, MA: Lexington Books.

Osborne, D. and Gaebler, T. (1992) *Reinventing government: how the entrepreneurial spirit is transforming the public sector from schoolhouse to statehouse, city hall to the Pentagon*. Reading, MA: William Patrick.

Ostrom, E. (1998) 'A behavioral approach to the rational choice theory of collective action.' *American Political Science Review*, 92(1): 1–22.

O'Toole, B. (2006) *The ideal of public service*. Abingdon: Routledge.

Pandey, S.K., Wright, B.E. and Moynihan, D.P. (2008) 'Public service motivation and interpersonal citizenship behavior in public organizations: testing a preliminary model.' *International Public Management Journal*, 11(1): 89–108.

Park, S.M. and Rainey, H.G. (2008) 'Leadership and public service motivation in US federal agencies.' *International Public Management Journal*, 11(1): 109–42.

Pautz, M.C. and Vogel, M.D. (2020) 'Investigating faculty motivation and its connection to faculty work-life balance: engaging public service motivation to explore faculty motivation.' *Journal of Public Affairs Education*, 26(4): 437–57.

Pedersen, L.H. (2014) 'Committed to the public interest? Motivation and behavioural outcomes among local councillors.' *Public Administration*, 92(4): 886–901.

Pedersen, L.H., Hjelmar, U. and Bhatti, Y. (2018a) 'What does the minister do? On the working conditions of political leaders.' *Public Administration*, 96(2): 259–75.

Pedersen, L.H., Pedersen, R.T. and Bhatti, Y. (2018b) 'When less is more: on politicians' attitudes to remuneration.' *Public Administration*, 96(4): 668–89.

Pedersen, L.H., Dahlgaard, J.O. and Pedersen, R.T. (2019) 'Rewarding the top: citizens' opposition to higher pay for politicians.' *Scandinavian Political Studies*, 42(2): 118–37.

Pedersen, M.J. (2015) 'Activating the forces of public service motivation: evidence from a low-intensity randomized survey experiment.' *Public Administration Review*, 75(5): 734–46.

Pedersen, R.T. and Pedersen, L.H. (2020) 'Citizen attitudes on politicians' pay: trust issues are not solved by delegation.' *Political Studies*, 68(2): 389–407.

Perry, J.L. (1996) 'Measuring public service motivation: an assessment of construct validity and reliability.' *Journal of Public Administration Research and Theory*, 6(1): 5–22.

Perry, J.L. (1997) 'Antecedents of public service motivation.' *Journal of Public Administration Research and Theory*, 7(2): 181–97.

Perry, J.L. (2014) 'The motivational bases of public service: foundations for a third wave of research.' *Asia Pacific Journal of Public Administration*, 36(1): 34–47.

Perry, J.L. (2021) *Managing organizations to sustain passion for public service*. Cambridge: Cambridge University Press.

Perry, J.L. and Porter, L. (1982) 'Factors affecting the context for motivation in public organisations.' *Academy of Management Review*, 7(1): 89–98.

Perry, J.L. and Wise, L.R. (1990) 'The motivational bases of public-service.' *Public Administration Review*, 50(3): 367–73.

Perry, J.L. and Hondeghem, A. (eds) (2008) *Motivation in public management: the call of public service*. Oxford: Oxford University Press.

Perry, J.L. and Vandenabeele, W. (2008) 'Behavioral dynamics: institutions, identities and self-regulation.' In J. Perry and A. Hondeghem (eds) *Motivation in public management: the call of public service*. Oxford: Oxford University Press.

Perry, J.L. and Vandenabeele, W. (2015) 'Public service motivation research: achievements, challenges, and future directions.' *Public Administration Review*, 75(5): 692–9.

Perry, J.L., Hondeghem, A. and Wise, L.R. (2010) 'Revisiting the motivational bases of public service: twenty years of research and an agenda for the future.' *Public Administration Review*, 70(5): 681–90.

Piatak, J.S. and Holt, S.B. (2020a) 'Disentangling altruism and public service motivation: who exhibits organizational citizenship behaviour?' *Public Management Review*, 22(7): 949–73.

Piatak, J.S. and Holt, S.B. (2020b) 'Prosocial behaviors: a matter of altruism or public service motivation?' *Journal of Public Administration Research and Theory*, 30(3): 504–18.

Plato. *The Republic.*

Pollitt, C. (2016) *Advanced introduction to public management and public administration.* Elgar Advanced Introductions Series. Cheltenham, UK: Edward Elgar.

Potipiroon, W. and Wongpreedee, A. (2020) 'Ethical climate and whistleblowing intentions: testing the mediating roles of public service motivation and psychological safety among local government employees.' *Public Personnel Management*, 50(3): 327–55.

Prebble, M. (2016) 'Has the study of public service motivation addressed the issues that motivated the study?' *American Review of Public Administration*, 46(3): 267–91.

Prosser, T. (2020) *What's in it for me: self-interest and political difference.* Manchester, UK: Manchester University Press.

Prysmakova, P. (2020) 'Contact with citizens and job satisfaction: expanding person-environment models of public service motivation.' *Public Management Review*, 23(9): 1339–58.

Rainey, H. and Steinbauer, P. (1999) 'Galloping elephants: developing elements of a theory of effective government organizations.' *Journal of Public Administration Research and Theory*, 9(1): 1–32.

Ribbins, P. and Sherratt, B. (2015) 'Centrism and the mandarin class: understanding the meta-politics of Whitehall bureaucratic neutrality.' *Public Policy and Administration*, 30(1): 5–30.

Riker, W. (1990) 'Political science and rational choice.' In J. Alt and K. Shepsle (eds) *Perspectives on positive political economy.* Cambridge: Cambridge University Press.

Riker, W. and Ordeshook, P. (1968) 'A theory of the calculus of voting.' *American Journal of Political Science*, 62(1): 25–42.

Ripoll, G. and Schott, C. (2020) 'Does public service motivation foster justification of unethical behavior? Evidence from survey research among citizens.' *International Public Management Journal.* DOI: 10.1080/10967494.2020.1825576

Ritz, A. (2011) 'Attraction to public policy-making: a qualitative inquiry into improvements in PSM measurement.' *Public Administration*, 89(3): 1128–47.

Ritz, A., Brewer, G.A. and Neumann, O. (2016) 'Public service motivation: a systematic literature review and outlook.' *Public Administration Review*, 76(3): 414–26.

Ritz, A., Schott, C., Nitzl, C. and Alfes, K. (2020) 'Public service motivation and prosocial motivation: two sides of the same coin?' *Public Management Review*, 2(7): 974–98.

Roman, A.V. (2017) 'The determinants of public administrators' participation in policy formulation.' *American Review of Public Administration*, 47(1): 102–29.

Ryan, R.M. and Deci, E.L. (2000) 'Self-determination theory and the facilitation of intrinsic motivation, social development, and well-being.' *American Psychologist*, 55(1): 68–78.

Saks, M. (2012) 'Defining a profession: the role of knowledge and expertise.' *Professions and Professionalism*, 2(1): 165–77.

Schillemans, T. (2013) 'Moving beyond the clash of interests: on stewardship theory and the relationships between central government departments and public agencies.' *Public Management Review*, 15(4): 541–62.

Schneider, B., Goldstein, H.W. and Smith, D.B. (1995) 'The ASA framework: an update.' *Personnel Psychology*, 48(4): 747–73.

Schott, C., van Kleef, D.D. and Steen, T. (2015) 'What does it mean and imply to be public service motivated?' *American Review of Public Administration*, 45(6): 689–707.

Schott, C., van Kleef, D.D. and Steen, T.P.S. (2018) 'The combined impact of professional role identity and public service motivation on decision-making in dilemma situations.' *International Review of Administrative Sciences*, 84(1): 21–41.

Schott, C., Neumann, O., Baertschi, M. and Ritz, A. (2019) 'Public service motivation, prosocial motivation and altruism: towards disentanglement and conceptual clarity.' *International Journal of Public Administration*, 42(14): , 1200–11.

Schubert, G. (1957) '"The public interest" in administrative decision-making: theorem, theosophy, or theory?' *American Political Science Review*, 51(2): 346–68.

Schuessler, A. (2000) *A logic of expressive choice*. Oxford: Princeton University Press.

Scott, P. and Pandey, S. (2005) 'Red tape and public service motivation: findings from a national survey of managers in state health and human services agencies.' *Review of Public Personnel Administration*, 25(2): 155–80.

Shaw, R. (2004) 'Shaping bureaucratic reform down-under.' *Commonwealth and Comparative Politics*, 42(2): 169–83.

Shughart, W. and Razzolini, L. (eds) (2001) *The Elgar companion to public choice*. Northampton, MA: Edward Elgar.

Simm, K. (2011) 'The concepts of common good and public interest: from Plato to biobanking.' *Cambridge Quarterly of Healthcare Ethics*, 20(4): 554–62.

Simon, H.A. (1947) *Administrative behaviour*. New York, NY: Free Press.

Simon, H.A. (1995) 'Rationality in political behavior.' *Political Psychology*, 16(1): 45–61.

Smith, A. (2006 [1759]) *The theory of moral sentiments*. Mineola, NY: Dover.

Somin, I. (1998) 'Voter ignorance and the democratic ideal.' *Critical Review*, 12(4): 413–58.

Stark, R. and Bainbridge, W. (1987) *A theory of religion*. New York: Peter Lang.

Sulkowski, L., Przytula, S., Borg, C. and Kulikowski, K. (2020) 'Performance appraisal in universities: assessing the tension in public service motivation (PSM).' *Education Sciences*, 10(7): 174.

Taylor, J. (2008) 'Organizational influences, public service motivation and work outcomes: an Australian study.' *International Public Management Journal*, 11(1): 67–88.

Tilburt, J.C. (2014) 'Addressing dual agency: getting specific about the expectations of professionalism.' *American Journal of Bioethics*, 14(9): 29–36.

Tullock, G., Seldon, A. and Brady, G. (2005) *Government failure: a primer in public choice*. Washington, DC: Cato Institute.

Tyran, J.R. and Engelmann, D. (2005) 'To buy or not to buy? An experimental study of consumer boycotts in retail markets.' *Economica*, 72(285): 1–16.

van Acker, W. (2020) 'Right-wing populist attitudes among European public servants: a cross-country comparison.' *Public Policy and Administration*, 35(4): 485–506.

Van de Walle, S. and Hammerschmid, G. (2011) 'The impact of the new public management: challenges for coordination and cohesion in European public sectors.' *Halduskultuur: Administrative Culture*, 12(2): 190–209.

van der Wal, Z. (2013) 'Mandarins versus Machiavellians? On differences between work motivations of administrative and political elites.' *Public Administration Review*, 73(5): 749–59.

Vandenabeele, W. (2007) 'Toward a public administration theory of public service motivation: an institutional approach.' *Public Management Review*, 9(4): 545–56.

Vandenabeele, W. and Jager, S. (2020) 'Government calling revisited: a survey-experiment on the moderating role of public service motivation in assessing employer attractiveness.' *Frontiers in Psychology*, 11.

Vandenabeele, W., Ritz, A. and Neumann, O. (2018) 'Public service motivation: state of the art and conceptual cleanup.' In S. Van Thiel and E. Ongaro (eds) *The Palgrave handbook of public administration and management in Europe*. London: Palgrave Macmillan.

Vogel, M.D. (2020) 'When service calls: public service motivation and calling as complementary concepts for public service.' *International Public Management Journal*. DOI: 10.1080/10967494.2020.1838014

Wang, T.M., van Witteloostuijn, A. and Heine, F. (2020) 'A moral theory of public service motivation.' *Frontiers in Psychology*, 11.

Ward, K.D. (2019) 'Suited to serve: the antecedents and perceptions of public service motivation in national service.' *International Public Management Journal*, 22(1): 71–98.

Ward, K.D. and Miller-Stevens, K. (2020) 'Public service motivation among nonprofit board members and the influence of primary sector of employment.' *Nonprofit and Voluntary Sector Quarterly*, 50(2): 312–34.

Weber, M. (1978) *Economy and society: an outline of interpretive sociology.* Berkeley, CA: University of California Press.

Weißmüller, K.S., De Waele, L. and van Witteloostuijn, A. (2020) 'Public service motivation and prosocial rule-breaking: an international vignettes study in Belgium, Germany, and the Netherlands.' *Review of Public Personnel Administration.* doi: 10.1177/0734371X20973441

White, D., Szabo, M. and Tiliopoulos, N. (2018) 'Exploring the relationship between narcissism and extreme altruism.' *American Journal of Psychology*, 131(1): 65–80.

Wilson, W. (1887) 'The study of administration.' *Political Science Quarterly*, 2(2): 197–222.

Wise, L. (2000) 'The public service culture.' In R. Stillman (ed) *Public administration concepts and cases.* Boston: Houghton Mifflin.

Wise, L. (2004) 'Bureaucratic posture: on the need for a composite theory of bureaucratic behavior.' *Public Administration Review*, 64(6): 669–80.

Wright, B.E. (2008) 'Methodological challenges associated with public service motivation research.' In J. Perry and A. Hondeghem (eds) *Motivation in public management: the call of public service.* Oxford: Oxford University Press.

Wright, B.E. and Grant, A.M. (2010) 'Unanswered questions about public service motivation: designing research to address key issues of emergence and effects.' *Public Administration Review*, 70(5): 691–700.

Wright, B.E., Christensen, R.K. and Isett, K.R. (2013) 'Motivated to adapt? The role of public service motivation as employees face organizational change.' *Public Administration Review*, 73(5): 738–47.

Wu, X.Y. and Jin, L.Y. (2020) 'Nudging: the unexpected impact on observers' inference of donors' prosocial behavior.' *Social Behavior and Personality*, 48(1): 1–8.

Yandle, B. (2011) 'Bootleggers and Baptists in the theory of regulation.' In D. Levi-Faur (ed) *Handbook on the politics of regulation.* Cheltenham: Edward Elgar.

Index

A

Abner, G.B. 26
accountability 65, 109, 124, 131
action and the public interest 56–8
advocates 9
affective motives 27–8
agency types 12
Akerlof, G. 113
Alcoba, R.C. 29
altruism 4, 29, 36–9, 69, 94,
 118, 119
 see also prosocial motivation
American political parties 15
Andersen, Lotte 29, 43, 45, 57, 66
Andreoni, James 4, 119
approval 5, 112, 141
Arrow, Kenneth 7
attraction-selection-attrition
 theory 28
autonomy 29
Awan, Sahar 30, 94–5

B

Bainbridge, W. 110
Becker, G. 110
behaviours
 altruistic and prosocial 37–9
 constraints on 3
 and decision-making 74–7
 and motivation 28
 of public servants 137
Belle, N. 13
benefits 11, 33
Bentham, Jeremy 55

Berg, J. 49
Black, Duncan 7
Blais, A. 10
Boruvka, E. 13, 41
bounded rationality 18, 19
Bozeman, Barry 29, 31, 44, 49,
 57, 59, 93, 95
 on public interest 51–4
 on public values 56–8
 Public values and public interest 53
Brewer, Gene 3, 25, 30–1, 35, 61,
 71, 93
Bright, Leonard 29, 59
Bromberg, D.E. 89
Brunnschweiler, C.N. 5
Buchanan, James 7
budget-maximisation
 theory 11–12
budgets 11, 12
bureau-shaping model 11–12
bureaucracy 8–12, 9, 56, 81
 senior bureaucrats 10

C

Caillier, J.G. 47
'call of public service' 1–4, 35, 46,
 51, 59, 105
Caplan, B. 5
Catalonia, research in 31
Charbonneau, E. 89
charitable sector 32, 35, 98
checks and balances 8
Cheng, K.T. 39, 63
Chong, D. 5, 112

Christensen, J. 54
Christensen, R.K. 39
citizenship behaviours 36, 39, 48, 60, 70, 92
  rights and obligations 57
civil service, view of the 20, 62, 65
'climbers' 9
Coase, Ronald 20
Cochran, Clarke, *Political science and 'the public interest'* 53
collective action 11, 17, 109, 126–7
  collective decisions 26, 123, 125
common good 1, 51, 54, 59, 125
communal narcissists 94–5
compassion *see* others, concern for
competence 29
competition 15, 55
  in government 8
  in the public sector 13
conflicts and motivations 100
conservatism 15
'conservers' 9
consumer boycotts 5
contract agencies 11
control agencies 12
Cooper, Christopher 39, 62
Cooper, D. 45
cooperation 5, 113, 126, 141
Cope, S. 10
Corduneanu, R. 29, 30, 39, 47
councillors 40
Coursey, D.H. 66
COVID-19 130
Crewson, P.E. 47
Cribb, J. 124
Croley, Steven P., *Regulation and public interest* 53, 56
cross-sectional surveys 95–9
Cruess, S.R. 43

D

Danish physiotherapists 44, 67–8
Davis, R.S. 39, 100
Dawson, C. 97
Deci, E. 28, 46, 47
decision-making 56, 65, 73–7, 108
  formal procedures in 55

localised 8
  and politicians 39
delivery agencies 11
democracy 53, 54, 62, 65, 66, 114
demotivation 97
Denmark, councillors in 40
Dion, S. 10
disabled people 39
disaggregation 13
Dollery, B. 12
Downs, Anthony 5, 7, 18–19, 120
  Economic theory of democracy 10, 40, 113–14
  Inside bureaucracy 9
Dunleavy, Patrick 12, 78–81
  Democracy, bureaucracy and public choice 9, 11

E

education 131
efficiency 16, 17
elections 62, 64, 65, 129, 131
Elster, J. 37, 110
emotions 108, 110
employment 30, 42, 97, 117
  benefits 9
  employee recruitment 28
  enjoyment at work 46, 107, 119, 128
  job satisfaction 19, 92
  job security 99, 117
  in the public sector 30–6
Engelmann, D. 5
environmentalist values 112
equity 16
Ertas, N. 97
ethics of public employees 16, 113
experimental designs 95, 98, 134
expressive motivation 110–13, 117–19
  and decision-making 122–7
  expressive generosity 130
  expressive rationality 5, 141
  expressive voting 113–15
  and PSMT 127–31
  and PSM testing 131–5
  and public employees 4–6
  and public interest 119–22
expressive policy traps 128–31

extrinsic motivation 46
extrinsic reward 17

F

Facer, R.L. 61
family, the 110
Fan, Y.M. 12
Fedel, Alessandro 40
Fennimore, Anne 37, 94
Ferlie, E. 13
Finkelstein, M. 48
firefighters 4, 31
Freidson, E. 42
Frey, Bruno S. 113, 128
    Not just for the money 47
funding grants 12

G

Gaebler, Ted, *Reinventing
    government* 16
Gailmard, S. 66
Gains, Francesca 12
Gans-Morse, J. 31
generosity 5, 141
goals 9, 18, 19, 107
    goal-orientated
        behaviour 111, 115
    goal theory 27
government 7, 11, 56, 108
    distrust of 15, 16
    elected governments 56, 62,
        66, 70–1
    government failure 8, 139
    government regulation 53
    quality of services 67
Grant, A.M. 47, 49, 93
Greece, Ancient 1
Green, D. 26
Greenwood, E. 42
group interests 55, 56, 63, 71

H

Hamburger, P. 12
Hamlin, A. 115, 117, 122, 134
Hammerschmid 14
Hantke-Domas, M. 54
Hartley, J. 57
Hayek, Frederick 20

health 131
    healthcare workers 31, 109
Hechter, M. 110
Held, V. 52
Herne, K. 18
Hillman, A.L. 5, 112–13, 115,
    123, 129, 130
Hindmoor, Andrew, *Rational
    choice* 19
Hodgson, G. 20
Holt, Stephen 31, 37, 38, 47, 97
homelessness 130
Hondeghem, Annie 17, 28, 29,
    32, 40, 63, 93
    *Motivation in public
    management* 46, 59
honesty 20
Hood, Christopher 13–14
Horton, Sylvia 1, 30, 65
hospital cleaners 42
Houston, David 47, 62, 63, 65
HS2 109

I

Iannaccone, L.R. 110
identifying motives, approaches
    to 134
identity 4–5, 107, 112, 119, 122,
    127, 134, 141
    and expressive utility 6
    and occupation 118
    professional 43, 45
    and public employees 72
ideology 54–5
impartiality 20
incentives and constraints 3, 18,
    79, 86, 110, 111, 112
income/pay 9, 10, 16, 46, 117
    performance-related pay 46
    private sector 124
individuals and organisations 29
individuals and self-importance 47
information problems 8, 18,
    63, 139
Ingrams, A. 48
institutional context 7, 29, 30,
    109
    institutional incentives 3
    institutional settings 124–5, 127

integrity 20
interests, different *see* group interests
International Management Journal 31
intrinsic motivation 5, 29, 46–9, 47–9, 112, 140
intrinsic reward 117

J

Jager, Stephanie 48, 69
Jankowski, Richard 37
Jasinenko, A. 57
Jennings, Colin 115, 117, 122, 126, 131, 134
Jensen, Ulrich 29, 40, 47, 67–8
Jin, L.Y. 48
John, Peter 12
Jordan, S. 53
Jorgensen, T.B. 57
journals 89

K

Kahneman, Daniel 20
Kanazawa, S. 110
Kerrissey, J. 39
Kim, Sangmook 30–5, 38, 47, 60, 70, 92, 97, 99
Kim, Seung Hyun 94
Kleiner, M. 45
Knoke, David 27
knowledge-based vocation 43
Koehler, M. 17, 47
Korea 92, 99
Kranton, R. 113
Krueger, Anne 7, 45
Kuo, N.L. 12

L

Lasswell, H. 39, 65, 108
Latham, Gary 27
left-wing 15, 66, 139
Le Grand, Julian 2, 62–3
Leisink, P. 28
liberalism 15
Liu, B.C. 32, 48
lockdowns 124, 130
Locke, Edwin 27
longitudinal research 92, 98
loyalty 19

M

MacDonald, K. 45
maintenance staff 42
management 13, 16
Manchester, homeless policy 130
markets 13
Massey, Andrew, *A research agenda for public administration* 35
Matthewson, D.J. 10, 12
McCarthy, D. 96
medical profession 42–3, 117
Meier, S. 49
methodology 87–8, 98
Meyer, R.E. 16
Meynhardt, T. 57
Miller-Stevens, K. 99
mixed motives 19, 45, 71, 99–100, 115–17, 127
Modarresi, S. 42
monopolies 7, 14
moral values *see* values
motivations and behaviour 107–8
motivations and settings 35
Myrdal, Gunnar 20

N

national security 57
Netherlands, politicians in the 40
Neumann, Oliver 30, 93, 119
New Public Management 13–20
and Public choice 17
Niskanen, William 7, 10, 13, 18–19, 63, 120
Bureaucracy and representative government 9
Nobel prizes 20, 110
non-work activities 48
Noordegraaf, M. 16
normative motives 27–8
normative consensus 56
public sector norms 125
Northcote-Trevelyn report 1854 20

O

objectivity 20
observational data 95
occupations 42, 117

O'Leary 3, 17, 20, 37, 52, 64, 93, 116
  on homelessness 130
  on professionalism 45
Olson, Mancur 7
  The logic of collective action 126
Ongaro, E. 13
Opp, Karl-Dieter 111
Ordeshook, Peter 114
Organ, D. 48
organisational incentive structure 28
Osborne, David, *Reinventing government* 16
Ostrom, Elinor 7, 18, 126
others, concern for 10, 17, 28, 32, 48, 100, 117
O'Toole, B. 1
outsourcing contracts 41
Oxford handbook of public choice 134

P

Pandey, S.K. 32, 59
Park, S.M. 47
partisan neutrality 65
patronage 10
Pautz, M.C. 89
Pedersen, Lene 40, 61
Pedersen, M.J. 127
Pedersen, R.T. 40
pensions 124
performance 16, 31
Perry, James 11, 28–9, 30, 31, 41, 47, 55, 93
  on identity 127
  Managing organizations to sustain passion for public service 27, 46
  The motivational bases of public service 2–3, 13
  Motivation in public management 46, 59
  on professionalism 43
  PSM measurement 35, 38, 60, 66, 92
  on the public interest 71
  on the public will 63
person-organisation fit 28
Phinaitrup, B.A. 29
physiotherapy 39, 44

Piatak, Jaclyn 31, 37, 38, 47, 97
Plato 1, 52
police officers 31, 91
policy 10, 26, 27, 32, 126, 128, 141
  and civil servants 65, 66–8, 71, 117
  implementation of 63
  policy traps 128–31
  and PSM 77–82
  and Public Choice 78–85
  research on 135
politics 1, 15, 52
  candidate motivation 40
  political behaviours 92, 139, 141
  political identity 112–13, 115
  political parties 113–15, 129
  politicians 39–42, 61, 70–1, 108
  politics-administration dichotomy 56, 64–8
Porter, L. 28
Potipiroon, W. 68, 100
power 9, 10, 19, 41
  professional 45
Prebble, Mark 15, 17, 29, 63, 66, 93
predisposition-opportunity theory 27–8
preferences 111
principal-agent problems 10
principles, set of 57
private schools 129
professionalism 16, 42–6, 118
prosocial motivation 48, 50, 69, 139
  prosocial behaviour 29–30, 36–9, 92, 97–8
  and rule- breaking 68, 70
Prosser, T. 113
Prysmakova, P. 89
psychological needs 29
public administration 13–20
Public Administration Review 94
Public Choice revolution 6–13, 55, 106
  and NPM 13, 17
  and policy making 78–85
public employees 3–4
  behaviours of 10, 137
  non-work activities of 32

and the policy making
   process 66–8
political bias of 66
and politicians 61
self-interests of 17
public institutions 2
public interest 28, 70, 137
   and action 56–8
   as an administrative process 55–6
   concepts of the 1–2, 52–4
   defining the 51–5, 68–70,
      120, 135
   furthering the 121–2, 124
   professions serving the 43–5
   and PSM 2, 19, 58–62
   *Public Personnel Management
      Journal* 94
publics, types of 55, 58–62, 63,
   71
public sector 108–9
   competition in the 13
public service
   the 'call' of 1–4, 35, 46, 51,
      59, 105
   and professionalism 42–6
public service motivation
   theory 2, 47, 137–9
   and altruism 36–9
   concepts of 25–30, 27–9, 29–30,
      93
   critique of 137–9
   and decision-making 73–7
   development of 6–13, 20–1
   and expressive
      motivation 127–31
   and identity 127–8
   and intrinsic motivators 49
   literature on 88–92
   as a middle range theory 26–7
   and NPM 17
   and the policy making
      process 77–82
   PSM measurement 13, 15,
      32–5
   and public interest 58–62
   and society 30–6
public services 2
   lower-cost 16
   and Public Choice 8
public stewards 62–4

public values approaches 56–8, 66,
   70, 139
public will, discerning the 57, 59,
   63, 66, 70

Q

quantitative methods 14, 87, 88,
   89, 91, 95, 98

R

Rainey, H. 17, 29, 47, 59
rational choice theory 4, 25,
   105–6, 110, 140
   and institutions 7, 11
   rational self-interest 12, 17–18,
      19–20
Razzolini, L. 7
Reagan, Ronald 2
real-world difference 26
reforms 13, 16, 17, 67
regulation 53
   of professions 45
   regulatory agencies 12
Reinagel, Tyler 62
relatedness 29
religion 110
research 91, 100
   agenda 87–92
   methodology 93–8
   public focus of 98–9
Ribbins, P. 12
right-wing bias 15
Riker, William 19, 114
Ripoll, G. 31, 99
Ritz, Adrian 3, 27, 39, 89, 92, 93,
   95, 99
Rome, Ancient 1
rules, breaking the 68
Russia, research in 31
Ryan, R.M. 28, 46, 47

S

Saks, M. 42
Schillemans, Thomas 62
Schneider, B. 28
Schott, Carina 29, 30, 48, 59, 99,
   120, 127
   on professional identity 43

on prosocial motivation 37–8, 68–9
Schubert, G. 56
Schuessler, Alexander 112, 115, 118, 121
Scott, P. 59
Selden, S.C. 61
self-determination theory 28–9
self-importance, image of 47
self-interest 9, 17
  and altruism 37
  of politicians 41
  and rationality 19–20
self-regarding behaviours 49, 107, 116–17
self-reporting 88, 93–5
self-sacrifice 28, 32–3, 38, 60, 118
Sen, Amartya 20
Serritzlew, Soren 43, 45, 120
service users 120, 121–2
  eligibility for services 75, 86, 121
  responsiveness to service users 16, 17, 39
Setala, M. 18
settings 35, 98
Shapiro, I. 26
Shaw, R. 12
Shughart, W. 7
Simm, K. 53
Simon, Herbert 18, 19, 20
Smith, Adam 110
social desirability bias 94, 94–5
social motives 27–9
social welfare 54
Somin, I. 5
Stark, R. 110
state, reducing the 8, 15
status and civil servants 9, 117
Steijn, B. 28
Steinbauer, P. 29, 59
students 91
Su, Xuhong 29, 31, 36, 44, 48, 59, 93, 95
Switzerland 92

T

taxation 15, 130
Taylor, J. 59

teaching 31, 117
tenure 125
Thatcher, Margaret 2
third sector 32, 98
Tilburt, J.C. 43
transfer agencies 11
trust 5, 62–3, 113, 141
Tullock, Gordon 7, 8
Twitter 112
Tyran, J.R. 5

U

United Kingdom 2, 12, 20, 65, 130
United States 15, 40, 89, 99
utility 4, 37, 79, 112
  expressive utility 122–3, 128, 129
  utilitarianism 54, 55
  utility function 19, 72, 106
  utility gain 113, 115
  utility maximisation 27

V

values 5, 20, 112, 122, 127, 139, 140
  of the public sector 16
  public values 48, 51, 57, 66
van Bockel, J. 16
Vandenabeele, Wouter 29, 30, 32, 48, 59, 69, 127
van der Wal, Z. 39, 40
Van de Walle, S. 14
Victorian era 20
Vogel, M.D. 29, 89
voluntary work 1, 39, 97
voters' mandate 56, 65
voting behaviours 5, 113–15, 131

W

Wang, T.M. 127
Ward, K.D. 99
'warm glow' see altruism
Weber, Max, Economy and society 63
Web of Science 88
welfare reform policy 130
Westminster model, the 65

whistle-blowing 39, 68, 70, 92
White, D. 37
Wilson, Woodrow 1, 56, 63
  politics-administration
    dichotomy 57, 64–8
Wise, Lois 11, 12, 17, 25, 27, 55,
  59, 93
  *The motivational bases of public
    service* 2–3
Wongpreedee, A. 68, 100
workers 42, 46

Wright, Bradley 47, 67, 95
Wright-Isak, Christine 27, 39,
  93
Wu, X.Y. 48

Y

Yandle, B. 52

Z

zealots 9

Printed and bound by CPI Group (UK) Ltd, Croydon, CR0 4YY

16/04/2025

14658339-0001